THE EVOLUTIONARY SELF
Hardy, Forster, Lawrence

Roger Ebbatson
Senior Lecturer in English,
Worcester College of Higher Education

HARVESTER PRESS . SUSSEX

BARNES & NOBLE BOOKS . NEW JERSEY

First published in Great Britain in 1982 by
THE HARVESTER PRESS LIMITED
Publisher: John Spiers
16 Ship Street, Brighton, Sussex

and in the USA by
BARNES & NOBLE BOOKS
81 Adams Drive, Totowa, New Jersey 07512

©Roger Ebbatson, 1982

British Library Cataloguing in Publication Data

Ebbatson, Roger
  The evolutionary self: Hardy, Forster, Lawrence.
  1. Darwin, Charles – Influence
  2. Evolution – History   3. Intellectual
  life – History
  I. Title
  941.081   QH31.D2

  ISBN 0-7108-0491-1

Library of Congress Cataloging in Publication Data

Ebbatson, Roger.
  The evolutionary self.

  1. English fiction – 20th century – History and
criticism. 2. Evolution in literature. 3. Darwin,
Charles, 1809–1882 – Influence. 4. Hardy, Thomas,
1840–1928 – Criticism and interpretation. 5. Forster,
E. M. (Edward Morgan), 1879–1970 – Criticism and
interpretation. 6. Lawrence, D. H. (David Herbert),
1885–1930 – Criticism and interpretation. I. Title.
PR888.E95E2 1982   823'.912'09356   82-8769
ISBN 0-389-20297-5   AACR2

Typeset in 11 on 12 Sabon by
Inforum Ltd, Portsmouth
Printed in Great Britain by
The Thetford Press Ltd, Thetford, Norfolk

THE EVOLUTIONARY SELF:
Hardy, Forster, Lawrence

FOR KATI

Contents

Acknowledgements

The author and publishers are grateful to the following for permission to quote from copyright material pertaining to D. H. Lawrence:

William Heinemann Ltd, Laurence Pollinger Ltd, the Estate of the late Mrs Frieda Lawrence Ravagli, and Viking Penguin Inc., New York, as follows:

Aaron's Rod   Copyright 1922 by Thos Seltzer Inc., renewed 1950 by Frieda Lawrence Ravagli.
Phoenix: The Posthumous Papers of D. H. Lawrence Copyright 1936 by Frieda Lawrence, renewed 1964 by the Estate of Frieda Lawrence Ravagli.
Phoenix II   Copyright 1959, 1963 and 1968 by the Estate of Frieda Lawrence Ravagli.
The Rainbow   Copyright 1915 by D. H. Lawrence, renewed 1943 by Frieda Lawrence Ravagli.
Sons and Lovers   Copyright 1913 by Thos Secker and Thos Seltzer Inc.
Women in Love   Copyright 1920, 1921 by D. H. Lawrence, renewed 1947, 1949 by Frieda Lawrence Ravagli.

To the following for permission to quote from copyright material pertaining to E. M. Forster:

Edward Arnold Ltd., W. Norton, Harcourt Brace Jovanovich, and Alfred Knopf Inc. as follows:
Arctic Summer
The Longest Journey
Maurice
Two Cheers for Democracy
A Passage to India

Introduction

It is a commonplace that evolutionary theory undermined the
certainties of Christian liberalism and ushered in a new phase
of aggressive social Darwinism or despairing neurotic sensibility. One of the most reputable accounts of the Victorian state
of mind speaks of the sense of isolation which a mechanistic
view of the universe produced, and describes Darwinism as
making 'an emotional impact more painful than madness or
bitterness — cosmic isolation and the terror of absolute
solitude'. This must have been true for many in an age of
doubt; but the argument of this study is that, by and large,
evolutionary theory acted as a creative stimulus to the
novelistic imagination. The language in which Hardy and
Lawrence speak of their reception of evolution is revealing.
Hardy, who ranked himself 'among the earliest acclaimers' of
The Origin of Species, quaintly described the effects of
Spencer's *First Principles*, a central document of the evolutionary movement, as 'a sort of patent expander'. The image of
liberation recurred in the next generation, when, as Jessie
Chambers recalled, the young Lawrence was deeply impressed
by this 'rationalistic teaching'. The effects on the writer's
imagination are nicely registered in her phraseology: 'He came
upon it at a time of spiritual fog, when the lights of orthodox
religion and morality were proving wholly inadequate, perp-
lexed as he was by his own personal dilemma.' This is the
language of deliverance rather than spiritual ordeal. Men left
without a metaphysic turned gratefully to evolutionism, which
in its pre-Darwinian form had certainly embodied an ideal of
progress. What the informed and careful reader of *The Origin
of Species* came to recognise was a world lacking in teleologi-
cal purposiveness, dominated by accident and chance, and yet
ecologically related and interdependent.

Whilst for many artists in the period what Darwin said was

less important than what he was thought to say, in the cases of Hardy and Lawrence the evidence of lengthy and detailed study of the theory is incontrovertible and becomes a defining characteristic of the novels themselves. A writer like Hardy was enabled creatively to restructure his imagination in the light of *The Origin of Species*, in a prolonged and seminal process of reorientation. Darwin's theory, as a type of scientific fiction, became a mental habit which enabled the generation of a new type of literary fiction. The unsatisfactory yet stimulating idea of mutation may be invoked in thinking of the afterlife of Darwin's thesis with its liberating influence. The novel as a form premises a self coming to grips with time and process, and the evolutionary perspective clearly presented the novelist with a new mode of handling temporal experience. Through a kind of ingestion, literature took into itself elements of an extraneous system which got expressed rhetorically through figurative devices, characterisation and structure. A novel like *The Woodlanders*, therefore, may validly be read as a work which translates Darwin into another medium. What follows is an attempt to trace the aesthetic revolution effected in the novelists' imagination, in what it became possible to conceive or to write, through the radiation of Darwinian theory.

The principal tenets of that theory were so widely known and yet so variably interpreted in the period that a brief summary is called for. In observing that plant and animal populations exhibited variation, Darwin discovered that some variations provide an organism with advantages over others in the 'struggle for life'. Such favourable variant types would, he foresaw, transmit advantageous characteristics to their progeny, and since populations tended to multiply rapidly, favourable variants would be numerically greater than unfavourable variants. Continuous evolutionary change in a population could then lead to the origination of new varieties or species under the impress of natural selection, which might be defined as a kind of sieve, a differential death-rate between classes of a population. *The Origin of Species*, in its sweep, ingenuity and subtlety, engaged the reader's mind with this coherent picture. Despite the improvisatory nature of Darwin's thoughts on inheritance, the general tendency of the work, the marrying of man back to his animal origins, represented the unsettling culmination of a long tradition of evolutionist thought. As Ruskin was to complain, 'You can't wash the slugs out of a lettuce without disrespect to your ancestors.'

Commitment to, or acceptance of, an evolutionary stand-point necessitated acceptance of the idea of instability of the present order and of the paradox that a change of state is the invariable characteristic of natural systems and human institutions. Intellectuals digesting the implications of the theory were constrained to accept it as a theory of knowledge, in the sense that it meant understanding change from one order to another. Many of them detected a sense of direction in this change — Spencer's 'beneficient necessity'. This may have been further than Darwin was willing to go: his concern, after all, had been with the mechanism of evolution. But the novelists considered in this study, like other writers of the period, inherited a shifting body of opinion rather than the theory outlined with such clarity in *The Origin of Species*. That shifting body of opinion fed in to new theories of the self, and notably into a diversity of theories of social and cultural evolution which would mark the course of fiction in the filigree of its shaping of character and environment from Hardy to Forster and Lawrence. Convinced of the orderliness of evolution, students of anthropology such as E.B. Tylor concerned themselves with world-wide manifestations of cultural stages rather than with the culture of particular societies. This theory had a unilinear quality in its stress on how certain stages of development could be traced universally; it also tended to encourage an organic model of society as a system of interdependent parts. In *Primitive Culture*, pub-lished twelve years after *The Origin*, Taylor posited a causal connexion between different aspects of culture, the determin-ing of cultural relations, and the thought-processes of the individual. This determinism reflected Tylor's thesis, which

Lawrence was to refract in *Women in Love*, that technology evolves independently of morals. In studying society in the light of Darwinism, social philosophers sought to distinguish those conditions which contained a potential for transformation from those that did not. In defining similarities amidst processes of growing differentiation, the concept of an élite of entrepreneurs capable of problem-solving was propounded and crystallised, notably by Weber, with his notion of the push given by charismatic groups. This is a complex of ideas which stands in close analogy to evolutionary mutation, and achieves its fictional apogee in Gerald Crich.

The range of applications of Darwin's theory shared with the theory the seminal concept of the species' adaptation to its environment. Evolutionary developments maintain the adaptedness of the species when the environment changes, or improve adaptedness where environment remains stationary. Both these patterns affect the novel of the period: in *The Woodlanders*, for instance, a relatively stationary environment allows the survival of dynamic types such as Fitzpiers; in *Jude the Obscure* the environment is changing rapidly, and here again the survivors are people not tragically compromised or torn apart by the incongruities of the evolutionary process. Environment, in the Darwinian reading, presents challenges to which living species may respond by adaptive modifications of their inherited nature. If the response is elicited, the species adapts and improves; if not, species may be faced with extinction. Evolution suggested that man's key adaptive trait was his educability, and Hardy, for instance, continued to believe in a progressive evolutionary potential into his old age. Nevertheless, in his tragic novels the opposing tendency in evolution, the sinking towards Spencerean 'dissolution' and extinction, creates a new structure of feeling with manifold possibilities for the future of the novel as an analysis of the self in society.

It should be admitted here that the texts under consideration may hold no necessary unity beyond that which is constructed by the critical discourse. The critique presented has the limited aim of identifying and elaborating certain problems and themes which are claimed to be internal to the texts within the prevailing ideology. The critical method used is thus, of necessity, one of relating the texture of a given novel, its language, imagery, characterisation, to a certain body of doctrine external to the novel itself. Justification for this strategy must lie in the degree to which the evidence and the argument are felt to be persuasive and illuminating in relation to this range of work. It is a method which involves a number of unresolved difficulties. A close working knowledge of a wide range of texts must be assumed, and the details of evolutionary theory must from time to time be wrenched from their proper scientific context to provide analytic tools for a fresh approach to some novels of Hardy, Forster and Lawrence. The risks inherent in such a procedure are self-evident – temptations to over-ingenious readings, importing of possibly irrelevant criteria, and the use of these classic texts as pegs on which to hang a thesis. Whilst such pitfalls may not have been wholly avoided, the study which follows ultimately rests its claim upon the simple proposition that evolutionary theory was of crucial significance in the imaginative life of the period, and that the structure and content of the novel, the way the novelist could perceive life, altered radically in response to the Darwinian revolution.

Evolutionary theory gave the writer a number of insights which he could use, notably the concept of struggle linked with man's animal past; the idea of vast stretches of time; and the alteration from fixed systems to a vision of development and process. Darwin, in his brilliant demolition of the idea of fixed species, unveiled a world in which essence is replaced by becoming, a world where there operates what Huxley designated 'a transitory adjustment of contending forces'. The notion of transition, of a world which was to be comprehended, as Engels wrote, not 'as a complex of ready-made *things*, but as a complex of *processes*', seminally affected the novelist's sense of the self and nature. The writer reading Darwin was made more critically aware of the biological

factors within the individual, and externally in his relation
with the environment. The terminology of the opposition
between individual and society, so brilliantly dramatised in,
for instance, *Wuthering Heights*, had now to be recast in terms
of heredity versus milieu, innate versus acquired, nature versus
nurture. The data exposed by Darwin and his explicators
enabled the novelist to examine the socialisation process in the
protagonist, a process in which biological factors would now
take precedence. Evolutionary theory, with its potent vocabulary of struggle, fitness and survival, was thus translated
into a kind of myth of origins whereby the contradictory
processes of socialisation and individuation could be
examined with a new sense of their complexity. Ursula
Brangwen is the supreme exemplar of this shift of perspective.
Indeed, in *The Rainbow* Lawrence grapples with the realisation that basic drives are located in the evolutionary analogy of
man with animal — the horses which threaten Ursula may be
taken as an exteriorisation of this inner primacy. The exploration of the biological nature of man is conducted in both the
Ursula section of *The Rainbow* and in *Jude*, where social
relations are increasingly felt as inimical to personal growth.
Hardy, Forster and Lawrence were thus led into the writing of
biographies which would study the way the self develops in its
relations and internal processes, working intensively upon
what has been termed the 'elaboration of the subject'. The
novelist, accepting many of the tenets of evolution, yet found
himself in a dilemma, since any positivist account of reality
claims to know that reality through its appearances. The
hegemony of positivism in this respect, the claim of science to
know, is challenged by the romantic imagination because of its
effects of 'freezing' the notion of character into a knowable
entity. Indeed it is just those characters who are positivists,
notably Gerald Crich, who undergo this stiffening to the
utmost and are abandoned by their creator. Hardy, Forster
and Lawrence were imaginatively quickened by scientific
rationalism whilst simultaneously refuting the literalism
which that tradition posits. Their characters, and the texts in

which they appear, must remain active within a web of possibilities. It is against the closure of these possibilities, the iron determinism of positivism, that Jude kicks. Lawrence's entire imaginative strategy may be read as an endeavour to redeem and preserve the mysteries of human character from the causation of science.

Such a sense of mystery especially surrounded the figure of the woman, and it is no accident that the self explored in this line of fiction should so frequently be female. In Hardy there is increasingly the feeling that the dominant patriarchal chain of authority oppresses women by enclosure, reducing them to silent mutes and observers (Marty South), or to Darwinian mimics (Arabella). The female, that is to say, fulfils roles given to her by men, and these roles are reinforced by language forms which reflect a sense that sexual differentiation is both natural and necessary. Attempts to define the female self in its mystery and singularity of evolutionary possibility in non-male terms lead to the strain of hysteria in Sue and later to the emergent conflict in Ursula. The perspective of change may be indicated by comparing organic and mechanistic accounts of life; Mill's words in *On Liberty* apply poignantly to such heroines:

Human nature is not a machine to be built after a model, and set to do exactly the work prescribed for it, but a tree, which requires to grow itself on all sides, according to the tendency of the inward forces which make it a living thing.

Yet these female protagonists, in their fluctuating vitality, are frequently crushed in a universe which more closely resembles a machine — the kind of world envisaged in D.F. Strauss's *The Old Faith and the New*, published in 1873, with its glance towards Tess's sufferings on the steam-threshing machine:

In the enormous machine of the universe, amid the incessant whirl and hiss of its jagged iron wheels, amid the deafening crash of its ponderous stamps and hammers, in the midst of this whole terrific commotion, man, a helpless and defenceless creature, finds himself placed, not secure for a moment that on an impudent motion a wheel may not seize and rend him, or a hammer crush him to powder.

It is precisely in the exploration of Mill's 'tendency of the inward forces' that the evolutionary novel excels, in its sensing, with Ernest Pontifex, that evolution works in mind as well as environment, and that transformations in the human will serve to break down taboo and custom. The position of women at this time served almost as a laboratory test for the Darwinian novelist, and the door which Nora slams at the end of *A Doll's House* reverberates through the fiction of the period. Its echoes are caught in such strange mutations as Sue's sacrificial opening of Phillotson's bedroom door or Ursula's fierce seaside destruction of Skrebensky.

Marx said that he aimed at self-change in human society, and this could stand as a motto within the novel at this time. Hardy felt that change was a sort of education, and his own predicament exemplified this insight. Whilst ethically and culturally holding on to Christian doctrine, ontologically and psychologically he responded to a wider collective experience which gained full tragic expression in the later novels. The common schema of the modern novel of a progression from a corporate traditional life towards competitive individualism is powerfully re-enacted in the sequential progression from *Under the Greenwood Tree* towards *Jude the Obscure*, where the narrator reflects that 'Every successful man is more or less a selfish man. The devoted fail.' The internal dislocations, stylistic lapses and incongruities of Hardy's style aptly reflect the need for a novelist nurtured as he was on evolutionary thought to tread warily between creating characters in whom either biological necessity or mental process is dominant. The split between Arabella and Sue, that is to say, dramatises some of the fissures in the authorial consciousness.

Coleridge justly observed that 'feelings die by flowing into the world of the intellect, becoming ideas.' With Hardy, Forster and Lawrence the dictum might be reversed: the propositions expounded by Darwin flowed into and became part of the novelist's imaginative equipment, part of his sense of self. Evolution, that is to say, came to be taken as a poetic construct or enabling myth which fertilised the novelist's imagination, just as the new romantic biology led to the sprouting organic life of art nouveau. It is not necessary to fall back on the false critical premise of the single unified interpretation to be able to argue that these novels may fruitfully be read within the evolutionary context. In a period of transition there will be a contradictory aesthetic unity of crisis and renewal, destruction and rebirth, and the evolutionary perspective perhaps enabled these writers to see themselves as the result of their own earlier work. This is very much the sense, for instance, of Lawrence's remarks on the work in progress on *The Rainbow*, when he talked of his 'transition stage' and of 'something deep evolving itself' within him. He was, both here and in *Women in Love*, evolving a style in which reality dissolves and re-forms itself before the reader's eyes, and his comment reveals his sense of each work as a fragment of meaning which would be fully clarified only when integrated into a larger perspective.

In Forster the evolutionary perspective, though present as a sub-text, is off-centre, and in his work may be discerned what has been termed 'the deviousness of the path of evolution'. *Maurice* specifically lies athwart complex cross-currents of the Edwardian evolutionary debate. That awkward novel, so directly and subtly issuing from the author's sense of self, is a lyrical story of the formation and deformation of the individual identity; it is a narrative which, because not fully articulated, is most powerful in its suggestive force as a text subversive of and hostile to the positivist tradition. Maurice is a man who is first of all 'constructed' by the determining world-view which surrounds him, which dominates and indeed creates him. Maurice goes beyond that construction and finds himself in conflict with existing structures both social and mental. The signficant form of *Maurice* is to be identified by locating the collective subject — the evolutionary controversy as brilliantly crystallised in Butler's quixotic Lamarckism. With characteristic indirection Forster here clashes with, and pierces through, the dominant consciousness of the period. Yet his inability to come to grips with social reality as something made by men and therefore changeable leads the novelist away from human statement towards self-fulfilling fantasy. Jude reflects that 'As you got older, and felt yourself to be at the centre of your time, and not at a point in its circumference ... you were seized with a sort of shuddering.' It is the fate of Maurice never to experience this shudder, but always to remain on the circumference, outside the ring-fence of society. Forster's work is an admissible and indeed exemplary protest, but *Maurice* remains obstinately a sport of the evolutionary debate explored, digested, rejected and rethought in Lawrence and Hardy with a higher degree of imaginative coherence and intensity. In *Tess* or *The Woodlanders*, *The Rainbow* or *Women in Love*, that is to say, the reader is confronted with a series of dramatic statements or representations which cohere into a block of meaning in which the implications of the evolutionary situation, positive and negative, are metaphorically dramatised and realised.

The novel is a structure which expresses human feeling, its rhythmic curves, troughs and crises; everything that may be designated the inner life is articulated by the novel to synthesise a sense of inner identity. That this mass of subjectivity required a structure was a problem for the novelist from Richardson onwards, and underlying the problem is the uneasy feeling that language somehow fails to meet the test, is not up to the job of reporting on the intricacies of the inner life. The patterns revealed to writers steeped in evolutionary theory enabled them to forge radically different objectifications of the inner landscape. In particular, the sense of self was notably extended by an understanding of organic process, of the way a creature utilises and replaces its own substance in a pattern of ceaseless change and renewal. Character typology met the challenge of Darwinism by imagining the self in terms of psychic changes, a functional identity inhering within another pattern of physical changes which move in a curve from growth to decay. The intricacy, complexity and interdependence of physical and psychic within evolution is recognised in the paradoxical tension in representative characters — Tess,

Sue, or Ursula — between their inviolability and fragility as separate selves. The assumption of bodily permanence which underlay the protagonists of earlier fictions — Emma Woodhouse, David Copperfield or Dorothea Brooke — gradually crumbles away into a new form of characterisation founded in periodic rhythm. Both the novel itself and the central figures took on a living form which began in the Darwinian matrix. Such a form went beyond the Romantic concern for organic structure: it perceived human life, and the art which sought to image that life, as a system of complex rhythmic processes of creation and disintegration. The need in Hardy or Lawrence is always to find a purposeful plot to embody the life of the self, since these writers perceive from their evolutionary reading a contradiction between characterisation of the self and a sense of purpose expressed in terms of plot. To imitate covert biological rhythms is inevitably to deny the terminus ad quem of Victorian plot structure because it coerces inner experience, and to seek to free the self from the warping tendencies of purpose. Sue Bridehead has no final goal: the realisation of her character must be entirely done in terms of perpetual transformation and fluctuation. The resistance of the self to form is amply registered in the wooden antitheses of *Jude the Obscure*, and it may have contributed to Hardy's abandonment of fiction. Lawrence takes up the anti-purposive stance in his essay on Hardy, where he praises 'extravagant being'. He is thus to be seen as taking Hardy's biological perception further, in his efforts simultaneously to recount a narrative and destroy the framework of the story. He does this, in *The Rainbow*, by breaking down what has been termed the 'genealogical imperative', allowing the actual family structure to crumble away as the narrative mode itself modulates in new directions. Ursula's acceptance of a self at the end is a rejection of family, education and culture in favour of growth and openness — the very principles of randomly determined life enshrined in Darwin's 'story'. If the defeat of Skrebensky is also a defeat of plotting, the struggle had to be renewed in *Women in Love*, where Gerald Crich seeks to impose his analytic and mechanis-

tic world-view. That view accords with readerly demands for
shape and plot, for the imposition of meaning on inchoate
experience, and Lawrence counters with the programme
enunciated by Birkin. The Lawrencean protagonist does not
wish to achieve brute mastery over life; rather he seeks
surrender to the river of dissolution and to the guiding
principle of randomness: 'Why strive for a coherent, satisfied
life?' he wonders. 'Why not drift on in a series of accidents —
like a picaresque novel?' The power struggle perceived by
Gerald is transmuted by Birkin into a comforting and
evolutionary vision of man's powerlessness: 'Whatever the
mystery which has brought forth man and the universe, it is a
non-human mystery, it has its own great ends.' Birkin, like his
creator, places his ultimate faith in 'the vast, creative, non-
human mystery'. The novel brilliantly enacts the tension
between these two variants of evolution, mirroring the
interplay between causation and randomness in its free yet
monolithic structure of scenic juxtaposition.

The chapters which follow seek to demonstrate the proposition that there is an evolutionary perspective of significance in
this group of texts, and that the novelists of these two
generations saw the world in terms of a model which they
articulate in a wide variety of ways. The area of exciting
discovery had partly shifted, since the eighteenth century, to
the life sciences, and *The Origin of Species* helped to inaugu-
rate a new age of biologism. The questionable employment of
biological theory about natural selection in fields unconnected
with biology drew its justification from Spencer, who had
detected in all cosmic process the operation of a single law of
evolution: the transformation of the homogeneous into the
heterogeneous. Evolutionary diction, imagery and assump-
tions subtly altered the mental landscape of the period,
enabling that landscape to accommodate such disparate
features as theories of eugenics, economic laissez-faire, and
cultural degeneration. The argument developed below is that
human character is for the first time in literature envisaged as
subject to the laws of biology, and that this realisation enabled

the novelist who had saturated himself in Darwinism to do something akin to what Zola claimed for naturalism — to make 'a totally new start' by 'getting to know man from the very well-springs of his being'. The limitations inherent in naturalism, the fact that, as it has been put, the 'theory of environment ends where the subconscious begins', may not so easily apply to the analogy of evolution, with its emphasis upon change and process. The manner in which phrases like 'struggle for existence' and 'survival of the fittest' enter the imagination of the period is a question of some complexity. Nevertheless, Darwin's incorporation of man into the process of natural selection would generate an imaginative response even where (or especially where) the novelist felt impelled to an act of rejection. The cluster of motifs which may be designated as evolutionary in these novels — survival, sexual selection, inheritance, individualism and collectivism, change, process and extinction — constitued an organic body of language, a new way of writing which subsumed a new way of seeing and experiencing reality. A theory about populations thus threw up patterns of meaning for literature. Cassirer has shown that art and science arise from a simple unified source, the motive for symbolic expression which finds its most profound manifestation in language. A crucial distinction, nevertheless, remains: the scientist like Darwin works always towards generalisation; the work of art is by definition specific. In the novels conceived under the impress of evolutionary theory the artistic problem resolves itself into a symbolisation of inner experience through imposition of abstract rhythmic form. Just as *The Origin of Species* may justly be designated profoundly concrete and abstract, so the evolutionary novel, working at its highest expressive pressure in these writers, is triumphantly abstract and concrete. It is the work of ensuing chapters to trace some of these patterns within the expressive integration of the text.

1   Hardy: The Complete Darwinian

I longed to love a full-boughed beech
   And be as high as he:
I stretched an arm within his reach,
   And signalled unity.
But with his drip he forced a breach,
   And tried to poison me.

I gave the grasp of partnership
   To one of other race —
A plane: he barked him strip by strip
   From upper bough to base;
And me therewith; for gone my grip,
   My arms could not enlace.

In new affection next I strove
   To coll an ash I saw,
And he in trust received my love;
   Till with my soft green claw
I cramped and bound him as I wove . . .
   Such was my love: ha-ha!

By this I gained his strength and height
   Without his rivalry.
But in my triumph I lost sight
   Of afterhaps. Soon he,
Being bark-bound, flagged, snapped, fell outright,
   And in his fall felled me!

('The Ivy-Wife', CP, 57)

Biology has often provided a seminal model for literature; romantic aesthetic theory and practice is notable permeated with vitalistic and organic metaphor. This early poem of Hardy's, cast as a botanical monologue, varies the classical trope of matrimonial bliss: the climber is a parasite which destroys its host and itself as lovers may destroy one another. The poem, which Emma Hardy read as a cruel attack upon herself, links natural and human worlds by transferring observable data about parasitism into the emotional and social life of humanity. It is a link Hardy would often make;

Mrs Charmond, for instance, relates parasitically with Little Hintock both as landowner and lover. In making such a transference the poet follows the lead of post-Darwinian monistic philosophy which stressed the universality of evolution and the unity underlying the diversity of nature. *The Origin of Species* itself had described the activities of parasites, Marx's 'ideologists of the vegetable world', and dealt in particular with the relationship between mistletoe and apple trees (*The Origin*, 116); this idea is translated directly by Hardy. The notions of unity and struggle are equally crucial: monism held that the individual viewpoint distorts reality, and that the world's apparent plurality stems from this confusion. Hardy's grasp of life was profoundly affected by this thesis. Writers of the period who digested Darwin gained an insight into human history as mechanism placed within a universal context — a perspective invaluable for a churchy agnostic novelist searching for a coherent secular order. Evolution might free the writer from the limitations imposed by the value-systems of his time as radically as subscription to Comteam or Marxist dialectic claimed to do. It is no accident that the female in this poem is the predator — the women in Hardy often act as unwitting carriers of destruction or subverters of promised happiness, and these tendencies culminate in the portrait of Sue Bridehead. Man, under the pressures of society, seeks to find authenticity in personal relationships which move against the constraints of that society. The pattern was available to literature before Hardy began writing (it dominates *Wuthering Heights*, for instance). But biological theory replaces the individual/society distinction with the more radical dichotomy of conscious motivation and mechanistic process. It is this distinction which, in *Jude the Obscure*, destroys man's most authentic private values.

Literature is neither biology nor philosophy but itself, and the impact of any body of dogma is judged by the literary coherence and intensity of the realisation in a self-contained unit of discourse. Hardy warned that writings spread over many years were not meant to yield a 'coherent scientific theory of the universe' (*Prose*, 49; 1911); they were, he insisted, 'seemings', 'a confused heap of impressions' (*Life*, 410; 1920). The notion of Hardy patiently sifting through the scientific evidence would be false to this outlook and to his shifty narrative stance, the acts of inattention through which he mediates his actions, and false also to the related instability of his style — an instability reflecting both uncertainty in Hardy about his public and private roles as a writer, purveyor of literary goods to be consumed in serial form, and the gradual disintegration of bourgeois values and writing styles in the late nineteenth century. Hardy's transactions with text and audience are liable to the widest variations of tone, intention and decorum. If the style is the man then Hardy is a man riven with irreconcilable contradictions. His language, in imposing shape upon reality, enacts these tensions, and the reader is in difficulty about fixing the identity of a narrator whose language flows from a contradictory mass of feelings, views and perceptions rather than from a coherent sense of self. Hardy's texts frequently disclose the multiple privacies of the man who hated to be touched, and enact ambiguities inherent in the conflict between desire and inhibition. Within this complexity of aesthetic purpose, evolution offered Hardy a code through which he could impose a pattern upon his universe.

The complex of ideas which may be designated evolutionary theory, understood as a Coleridgean 'fiction of science', worked often at subconscious levels in Hardy's imagination, and through it he gained a new way of seeing human and natural orders. By a vocabulary of equivalence a world is presented which is dominated by evolutionary law. The interconnexions between Hardy's creativity and the social thought of the age exist not only on the level of content but as categories which structure both fictional and evolutionary 'worlds'. Whilst it sometimes happens, especially in the philosophical poems, that Hardy resorts to cosmic simplifications which become inflexible carriers of prejudice, his best art is marked by a plasticity which recreates and redefines this body of doctrine in human terms. Reading Darwin gave Hardy a mode of representing a felt reality; far from becoming addicted to a mechanical idea of fate, his imagination was germinated by evolutionary theory in ways from which he was temperamentally disposed to benefit. The poet, Hardy felt, 'should express the emotion of all the ages and the thought of his own' (*Life*, 386; 1918). In coming to terms with currents of scientific rationalism Hardy was at odds with contemporary aesthetic movements; his work treads warily between the symbolist prescription that rational discourse give place to self-authenticating image, and naturalism with its 'need to analyse in order to know'. Cultivation of the aesthetic stance was an artistic strategy adopted to undermine the hegemony of materialism. Yeats condemned the 'brooding over scientific opinion that so often extinguished the central flame in Tennyson', but it was precisely such brooding which aided the formation of Hardy's imaginative world. The modernist distinction between the man who suffers and the mind which creates is irrelevant to Hardy. On the contrary it is assumed in his work that, in order to maintain a committed interest in life, literature must engage creatively with serious thought. The artistic problem, unsolved in the philosophical poems but resolved in the mature novels, is that something be done with the doctrine. When evolutionary theory is fully integrated and expressed in the texture then discourse and symbol coexist — the climactic scenes of even an early novel like *Far from the Madding Crowd* bear this out. If the novel is indeed the private experience of society, still that experience will also reflect, reformulate, reject, decompose and re-form the ideas of the time. As Hardy acknowledged in 1891, 'with our widened knowledge of the universe and its forces, and man's position therein, narrative, to be artistically convincing, must adjust itself to the new alignment' (*Prose*, 135). This openness to evolutionary doctrine is followed through heuristically in the novels, which evolve both in themselves and within the series from *Desperate Remedies* to *Jude the Obscure*. So radical an openness would disable Hardy from creating a Des Esseintes or Stephen Dedalus; conversely the aesthetic movement, for whom scientific prose registered a universe of death, was unable to body forth a Clym Yeobright, Angel Clare or Sue Bridehead, figures known to 'the pitch of saturation' in whom the ache of modernism is archetypally felt. Whilst Hardy retained traditional narrative procedures and comforted himself with the humbling reflection that all story writers were Ancient Mariners, his complex response to crises both scientific and marital led his art forward into ever deepening insights and dramatisations; the immediate social and economic realities of agricultural distress take their place within this wider perspective of time. Such a shift can yield complacency and muddled thinking, but may also lead to a more profound human awareness; the resultant discrepancies constitute part of the rewarding puzzle of the characteristic Hardy text.

Readers of Hardy recognise what they take to be a basic pessimism in the cosmic view, as in these verses from 'In a Wood' (*CP*, 64):

Heart-halt and spirit-lame,
  City-opprest,
Unto this wood I came
  As to a nest;
Dreaming that sylvan peace
Offered the harrowed ease —
Nature a soft release
  From men's unrest.

But, having entered in,
  Great growths and small
Show them to men akin —
  Combatants all!
Sycamore shoulders oak,
Bines the slim sapling yoke,
Ivy-spun halters choke
  Elms stout and tall.

The poem rejects what Hardy took to be the Wordsworthian position and states his own Darwinism, with its insistence upon combat as a valid metaphor for life. It is a poem which raises the question of what Hardy derived from Darwin's thesis, and how his creative misreading of that thesis was transmuted into the stuff of fiction. A range of arbitrary categories may clarify this question, with the proviso that it is not possible to draw an accurate line between what Darwin thought and what his work allowed others to think — what was borrowed from, or lent to, the naturalist's theory. Like any original postulate, what T.H. Huxley designated Darwin's 'essentially new creative thought' had to be comprehended in the light of contemporary ideology.

I Process and Change

Classical evolution theory differed from the eighteenth-century notion that evolution was a literal unfolding of what was pre-formed, like the fiddle-head of a fern. Darwin did not use the word evolution in the 1859 first edition of *The Origin of Species*; the key definition was to come in Spencer's *First Principles* of 1862, where the process was defined as a change from indefinite incoherent homogeneity to definite coherent heterogeneity through continuous differentiation effected by external pressures. Evolution thus came to denominate organic change through transmutation, and its essence was the concept of change, or more accurately a number of differential rates of change, which governed all matter. That is central to Hardy; it gives him his sense of human littleness, a vast perspective on human affairs, and also provides a model for understanding social and human developments. The ongoing movement may be felt as bringing pain; it was the 'becoming' of the world, Hardy once remarked, 'that produces its sadness'. 'If the world stood still' then 'there would be no sadness in it' (*Life*, 202; 1887). That remark implies a backward glance to versions of pastoral no longer available to a writer in late-Victorian agricultural Wessex. Even *Under the Greenwood Tree*, which comes closest to pastoral, shows how family and rustic pieties were interpenetrated by the historical continuum: Dick, with his vain and educated wife, will be a different type of tranter from his father. But the disabling melancholy of Hardy's remark, though an indisputable feature of his work, is less vitally connected with his successful fiction than his conception of history as process, 'rather a stream than a tree' (*Life*, 172; 1885), in the Arnoldian current of which both society and human personality must change and evolve. The tragic personalities of the fiction are rooted in unconscious life-processes but attempt to mould their lives by human will and aspiration; their acts of self-assertion are obliterated by cosmic process. Drama in a Hardy novel is engendered by 'the WORTHY encompassed by the INEVIT-ABLE' (*Life*, 251; 1892). Man shares in biological processes, most strikingly for the novelist in his sexual drives; but the aspiration of humanity which separates him from the natural creation endows his defeat with an inherent nobility, and sometimes with a 'founding hope' for the future which might justly be termed evolutionary meliorism.

However, the emphasis is not always upon process as engendering tragic defeat of human purpose. In other ways change as inevitable process brings about new conditions and opportunities such as occur in natural evolution. Engels justly perceived how evolution revealed 'that the world is not to be comprehended as a complex of ready-made *things*, but as a complex of processes': by dissolving the 'counters and fixities' of older systems of thought evolution released the perceiving mind in Hardy and enabled him to read his society with greater insight. The changes in the countryside around him were manifold: from labour-intensive farming to mechanisation; from high capital outlay to retrenchment; from monopoly to international competition; from part-payment in kind to payment in cash for labourers; from subsistence farming to business farming, and so on. Writing on the situation of the Dorset labourer Hardy noted that 'Change is also a certain sort of education' (*Prose*, 180; 1883), and the implications of this remark are everywhere in the later fiction. Society and the individual may be thought of as evolving at different rates, and the individual himself may be riven with internal contradictions: Hardy notes with interest how Phillotson and Gillingham, though 'well-trained and even proficient masters', 'occasionally used a dialect-word of their boyhood to each other in private' (*JO*, 250), past and present here co-existent in a confusing simultaneity epitomised by cultural sedimentation of the language. Hardy's novels cover a critical period of transition in Wessex which an understanding of evolution theory, translatable into analysis of the 'metamorphic classes of society' (*HE*, 320), helped him to comprehend. Change as education is continually present in the novels: Tess, by studying to Standard Six under a London teacher, is already removed from her mother's 'fast-perishing' world by a gap of two hundred years (*TD*, 50), and this education would have given her upward mobility in the class structure had it not been for the 'liberal education' afforded by her seduction. Grace Melbury takes advantage of her uprooting from the Hintocks to marry into another niche in society than her father's. In many such cases Hardy explores the notion that literacy may be a divisive agency. To move from one niche to another is to adapt successfully, as for instance the birds took over the air from the flying reptiles; but the progressive tendencies of this type of movement, though welcomed theoretically by Hardy, bring hidden strains and tensions. Evolution became a model for social change by showing how patterns could be traced in an evolving culture. Rapid social change would begin to obliterate traditional areas of experience across the board from spiritual values to work norms. Furthermore, Darwinism enabled the artist to grasp the idea that change in a group, class or society was not explicable solely by reference to a mono-causal external agency (for example, the effects of the weather on the denizens of Casterbridge in *The Mayor*). Internal factors were acting continuously to promote social and economic change, and personal structures of feeling would alter to accommodate such changes — this leads to the neurosis of Angel Clare or Sue Bridehead, both of whom seem to be undergoing strange mutations in their affective life. It was not necessary to hold that consciousness inheres in the material base to perceive that forces of change were inevitable

and critical, and that ideology and art would relate dialecti-
cally to those forces. Evolutionary theory could be read as a
conflict model without reference to Marx, and it could
analogically account for change as response to both internal
contradictions and strains and to external agencies. But it also
stressed continuity: Darwin insisted that nature does not make
leaps. Applied to Wessex this would explain how factors like
industrialisation, urbanisation, literacy expansion and occu-
pational mobility would subtly or overtly alter value-systems,
relationships and ultimately consciousness: Tess is caught out
in a society in which there can be no common ground between
Dairyman Crick and Angel Clare; the co-operative feudal
labour of harvesting at Marlott is replaced by capitalist
mechanisation of agriculture at Flintcomb-Ash as surely as
religious orthodoxy was being undermined by *Essays and
Reviews*. Hardy lived this experience, and pertinently
remarked the disappearance of what he called the 'two distinct
castes' of the village: artisans, traders, craftsmen, liviers and
manor-house servants; and farm labourers. The complexity is
well registered by his remarks on the facts of uprooting and
material improvement in the labourer's lot, and by his
attentive delineation of the endurance of conviction, the way
in which the material culture changed more quickly than
value-systems, beliefs and modes of self-definition. The sensitivity to differential rates of change, as for instance, the
steady decline of rural population in the latter part of the
century set against the rapid advance in technology, is central
to Hardy's art: he treats such changes comically, in the
obsolescence of the Mellstock Quire and its replacement by
the new-fangled organ played by a 'successful rival' (*UGT*,
179); tragically, in the death of old South; or neutrally, as in
the portrait of young Avice, 'a girl who with one hand touched
the middle-class and with the other the rude and simple
inhabitants of the isle' (*WB*, 164). Such alterations of state are
internal. The career of Gabriel Oak traces a graph between the
economic axes of dependant and employer. At the opening of
the novel he is getting known as Farmer Oak, as lessee of a

small sheep-farm; he has risen from shepherd to bailiff to farmer, only to sink again to hired hand through the ill-fated enthusiasm of his young dog. The stability and persistence which his name guarantees are in marked contrast to the economic and social uncertainty even of the stable agricultural order celebrated in *Far from the Madding Crowd*.

The human group in Wessex is not a tabula rasa upon which external influences are automatically registered. The patterns of cultural response to economic change range from continuity to transformation — a range embodied in the contrast between *Far from the Madding Crowd* and *Jude*. Such cultural responses include transvaluation, whereby traditional symbols acquire new meaning, and substitution, whereby contemporary society from the metropolitan centres absorbs traditional ingredients. Social patterns develop in unforeseen ways, and yet social processes do not lack structure. Changing links of interdependence will alter the balance of power in a community, with new constraints but also new options for the individual and resulting changes of allegiance. These simple notions are fleshed out in the Wessex novels, but if the focus there falls upon 'country customs and vocations, obsolete and obsolescent', as Hardy wrote in his General Preface to the novels in 1911 (*Prose*, 46), the wider implications of evolution are not forgotten. The reader's sense of some of Hardy's most powerful figures gains resonance from Marx's observation that 'men make their own history, but they do not know that they are making it.'

When biology is taken as model for social change, as Spencer proposed to take it, the danger is that a confusion of scale takes place whereby the biological model becomes so diffuse that it explains nothing which is happening to people in a society at a given moment. Cosmic scale offers an escape from having to think out the implications of human suffering on a daily basis. Hardy falls into this confusion of scale, and it takes the form with him of an engulfing objectless melancholy which blurs social reality. His self-regarding cosmic perspective, paraded frequently in the philosophical poems, is essentially escapist — Hardy does not wish to see what has happened to himself or the people around him and takes refuge in a fiction of private loss or family curse projected out onto the universe at large. A similar failure to define forces of change vitiates the novels locally. Clym Yeobright's educational plan for Egdon is put forward as the activity of a 'future type' with little perception of how, if successful, such a scheme would engender conflict between tradition and awakened aspiration. Less seriously, the woodenly plangent use of the new astronomy in *Two on a Tower*, and the exclamations about the terror and immensity of space, bury the interestingly mobile status of the hero and the feminist potential of the heroine beneath a sensationalist plot. A similar cosmic perspective is incongruously invoked in the conversation between Tess and Abraham about the earth as a 'blighted star', an exchange which, like the later garden-scene, arises directly out of Hardy's engagement with the evolutionary debate since it shows him recalling some words he had earlier copied out from a review of Francis Galton's *Inquiry in Human Faculty and Development* of 1883:

We perceive around us a countless number of abortive seeds and germs; we find out of any group of a thousand men selected at random, some who are crippled, insane, idiotic, and otherwise incurably imperfect in body or mind, and it is possible that this world may rank among other worlds as one of these.

(*Literary Notes*, 160)

Whilst he was always liable to reproduce this kind of undigested evolutionary speculation, Hardy's mature reflections on his pertinaciously veiled social origins and his more disinterested witness to complex agricultural movements in rural Dorset at a time of depression gave his novels an increasingly high social definition. The temptations to fudge class conflict and social divisiveness, economic exploitation and sexual egotism grew less under the sense of 'the mutations so increasingly discernible in village life' (*TD*, 400), as a comparison between an early and a late novel will show.

In his first large-scale novel, *Far from the Madding Crowd*,

Hardy skirts round the issue of an evolving society in the interests of the fable. Although the date of the action is unclear, it certainly lies within the period 1850–70. This was the era of high farming based on the Norfolk rotation method whose end-products were wheat, barley and sheep — the staple of the Weatherbury farms. The shepherd's role was vital to this economy; his status was defined by his practical skills, and most shepherds were illiterate. Hardy bowed to audience expectations by giving Oak an implausible amount of book-learning and by paring down the dialect formations of his speech whilst the serial version was in proof. The focus in the novel is upon the yeoman-class of tenant-farmers, and the landed gentry are carefully excluded. Hardy later claimed that he wrote 'from the point of view of the village people themselves instead of from that of the Hall or the Parsonage', but the overall effect in *Far from the Madding Crowd* is of a reduction of the arena of class tension and the creation of an aura of immemorial stability. This aspect is embodied both in the ancient buildings which define the social pattern — farmhouse, church, barn, malthouse — and in the seasonal agricultural activities. Yet as Hardy was writing *Far from the Madding Crowd* high farming was in collapse, its profitability undermined by bad seasons and overseas competition, and the 'Revolt of the Field' was at its height. Living at Bockhampton, in one of the lowest-paid agricultural counties, Hardy witnessed at first hand this upheaval with its causal connexions in agricultural depression, land reform and rural exodus. *Far from the Madding Crowd* averts its gaze from change and conflict and memorialises a communal way of life designed to appeal to the middle-class readership of the *Cornhill*, that 'stupid public' Leslie Stephen both deplored and subserved, an audience not merely consuming but participating in the creation of the code of the novel by demanding novels fashioned in their own image. The stress upon community echoes the ideology of a landed class who might appeal to such a mythical concept to maintain the stability essential to profitable farming, stability rooted in the class system which legitimised the principle of inherited authority by defining the workers' role and values for them. The 1870s saw the power of the squirearchy undermined by market forces and rural unrest; in economic terms the entrepreneurial replaced the aristocratic in just the way the specious d'Urbervilles establish themselves at the Chase. By scrupulously excluding the owners of land, and by placing the action in a vaguely recent past, Hardy offered comfort to his readers; they could enjoy the picture of a static agricultural order, overlooking the fact that such an 'order' arose as a result of the recent historical process of enclosure. Yet at the same time he allows the force of sexual selection full play with its mismatching and deadly rivalry (Oak's asexual standing aside reflecting that here Hardy attempts a partial portrait of his father). On the personal level evolutionary effects are registered; on the social and economic level they are quietly censored. The agricultural depression was a phenomenon of change which was made up of the experience of thousands of individuals who faced financial ruin and altered social status often without comprehension. Hardy's censorship was perpetrated most notably on the 'rustic chorus' (the name may stand as reflecting something of Hardy's own attitude at this period). The class-solidarity of the tap-room, and the infiltration into isolated villages of unionist ideas — all the subversive activities of what has been termed the 'dark village' in contradistinction to the 'official village' — these factors for change are deleted in favour of a gallery of Shakespearean characters presented with all the acuteness of Hardy's idiosyncratic mode of regard. This chorus is as deferential to the status quo as the Chickerel brothers in Hardy's subsequent novel, with their creepy determination not to compromise their sister by acknowledging her in public. The author, who counted himself a radical on the strength of 'The Poor Man and the Lady', appears to endorse the brothers' view that 'any man will touch his hat for a pint of beer' (*HE*, 125). On the other hand, it is clear with regard to *Far from the Madding Crowd* that the incidence of depression in Dorset was highly variable and dependent upon landlord attitudes and individual skills in farming. This might justify the way the sexual and psychological drama is played out against a backdrop of unchanging seasonal activities and rustic certainties. Despite the static society envisaged here, it is a mark of Hardy's genius that *Far from the Madding Crowd* richly sustains the illusion of a lived reality. But the illusion could not be kept up; in later rural novels Hardy would no longer ignore social evolution through conflict in the community on his doorstep. In *Tess*, *The Mayor of Casterbridge* or *The Woodlanders* personal griefs and obsessions unite with a deeper awareness of the dynamic forces of social evolution at work in agricultural society at large and in the individual lives making that society.

The Woodlanders, for example, holds a fine balance in its portrayal of both perspectives, the overall drive of evolutionary struggle which dominates the setting and action, and the economic cross-currents set up in an isolated rural community by educated social mobility. The range of Hardy's vision and the sureness of touch are remarkable: he encompasses uprooting of ancient homesteads and lives (the Souths, Winterborne), the ambitions of a rising middle-class (Melbury), the impact of metropolitan education (Grace, caught, like her creator, 'in mid-air between two storeys of society'), bogus intellection (Fitzpiers), and parasitic upper-class idleness (Mrs Charmond), all inhering in the economic base provided by the woodlanders themselves. The entire range of characters intersects through the socially indifferent force of sexual attraction. Here the evolutionary perspective is aptly scaled down and applied to the human group; the tinge of romanticisation in the delineation of Oak or Venn gives place, as in the later sketch of Tess at Flintcomb-Ash, to the endless round of labour and the sufferings of Winterborne and Marty. Comparison of early and late novels demonstrates a radical alteration in the horizon of expectations: each new literary text evokes for the reader a horizon of expectations and rules familiar from earlier texts which are variously reproduced or altered. In *Far from the Madding Crowd* or the botched ending of *The Return of the Native* the aesthetics of audience reception determine form and content; in *The Woodlanders* or *Tess* the horizon of expectations is that of a small group of 'advanced' readers, forerunners of a more enlightened younger generation which would include Jessie Chambers and D.H. Lawrence.

II   Chance

Darwin stressed that random modifications of species were how change occurred; these were then 'tested' by the environment in the 'struggle for existence'. Without genetics Darwin could not accurately account for this activity. Modern biology distinguishes between genotype, the chance genetic structure, and phenotype, the visible character which is determined by selection. Nonetheless Darwin's incomplete argument was sufficiently cogent to impress a mind like Hardy's with the image of nature dominated by chance mutations:

How arrives it joy lies slain,
And why unblooms the best hope ever sown?
— Crass Casualty obstructs the sun and rain,
And dicing Time for gladness casts a moan . . .
These purblind Doomsters had as readily strown
Blisses about my pilgrimage as pain.

('Hap', *CP*, 4)

In several poems Hardy ponders the idea that design has been removed from the world and that there is no beneficent creator or anthropocentric universe. Darwin pointed out that 'one grain in the balance will determine which individual shall live and which shall die' (*The Origin*, 442); and Spencer noticed how the 'tenor of a life may be changed by a word of advice; or a glance may determine an action which alters thoughts, feelings, and deeds throughout a long series of years' (*Principles of Biology* I, 265). This struck home and ramified into Hardy's plot structure; although his plots may reveal his modest desire to prove himself a 'good hand at a serial' (*Life*, 100; 1874), they also mirror the randomness of nature itself, expressive of 'Life's lottery' in which the dice 'fling no prize'

('Sine Prole', *CP*, 722). The coincidences, accidental encounters, mysterious ties of kinship, broken appointments and lost letters notorious with Hardy are a mode of dramatising the vital element of chance in the creation and survival of species and individuals, especially in its matching and mismatching of the sexes. This is the world in which, as Engels observed, 'the so-called accidental is the form behind which necessity hides itself.' Hardy's eye is held obsessively on what is called, in *The Mayor*, 'contrarious inconsistencies' in nature which baffle and ultimately defeat; the final paragraph of that novel speaks of the 'persistence of the unforeseen', and this provides the key to the foregoing action rather than the defeatism of the last phrase about a 'general drama of pain'. Hardy's conception of chance is nicely rendered in the dicing scene in *The Return of the Native* between the reddleman and Wildeve — the human figures in a pool of light provided by the glow-worms and surrounded by the darkness, the contrast rendered in its shifting complexity by the distinction between the human greed of Wildeve and the timid curiosity of the heath ponies at which he throws stones (a distinction made earlier in Hardy when the workhouse officer stones the dog which befriends Fanny Robin). The implications of the dicing scene are that men are 'bond-servants of Chance' ('Ditty', *CP*, 18), and should be prepared, like Clym, to 'abide by the game' (*RN*, 230), participants in an evolutionary game of chess in which, as Huxley observed, to 'the man who plays well, the highest stakes are paid', whilst those who play badly are 'checkmated' (*Science and Education*, 1897, 82). Chance will also enter into and affect structure. Hardy loved the 'cunning irregularity' of Gothic (*Life*, 301; 1899) and reproduced it both in his 'inexact rhymes and rhythms' (*ibid.*, 105; 1875) and in his large-scale plotting. It is the quadrille-like precision of antitheses in *Jude*, what Hardy designated its ' "rectangular" lines' (*Letters* II, 105; 1896), which vitiates the full impact of that dramatic conception. As Hardy noted during the composition of *Tess*, 'Art is a disproportioning . . . of realities' (*Life*, 229; 1890).

III Evolution of Consciousness

Hardy extrapolated from *The Origin of Species* what Darwin did not say: that evolution brought unhappiness because human beings had attained 'a degree of intelligence which Nature never contemplated when framing her laws, and for which she consequently has provided no adequate satisfactions' (*Life*, 163; 1883). The Spencerean First Cause was 'neither moral nor immoral but *un*moral', and thus human emotion and aspiration had 'no place in a world of defect, and it is a cruel injustice that they should have developed in it' (*Life*, 149; 1881), and that 'the disease of feeling germed' ('Before Life and After', *CP*, 277). This feeling was widespread. In 1897 Conrad remarked how life, 'the infamous thing', made itself 'without thought, without conscience, without foresight, without eyes, without heart. It is a tragic accident — and it has happened.' By gradually uncovering 'the defects of natural laws', Hardy held, men would find themselves in a quandary which science was powerless to resolve (*RN*, 191). The unplanned emergence of consciousness in nature, leading man to find 'blemish/Throughout [her] domain', as nature concedes in 'The Mother Mourns' (*CP*, 112), must often cause a disjunction between man and environment, and the novels frequently resound to 'The mortal moan/Begot of sentience' ('The Aërolite', *CP*, 770). *Jude the Obscure* best illuminates the gradually overwhelming sense in the later novels of 'Nature's indifference to the advance of her species along ... civilised lines' (*Life*, 405; 1920): both Sue and Jude possess potential for human transformation to a new 'type', but the actualisation breaks them. The increasingly alienated consciousness of Hardy himself may be plotted in the fiction moving away from the folk consciousness embodied in Jemima Hardy and crystallised in *Under the Greenwood Tree* and *Far from the Madding Crowd* towards the urbanised deracination of *Jude*, the tearing up of the 'pact of generosity' with his readership, the retreat from writing as a social act to the privatised form of poetry, and the consequent extinction of the writer as novelist.

IV   Struggle and Competition

Darwin said that species developed from common stock by variation and that possession of certain qualities would aid breeding success which was the key to survival. Evolution theory is about populations and breeding, but the Victorian general reader, misled by Darwin's terminology, gave his fullest attention to the sense of struggle in nature. As Hardy sometimes perceived it, nature resounded to the sound of 'Strange orchestras of victim-shriek and song,/And curious blends of ache and ecstasy' ('The Sleep-Worker', *CP*, 121). Hardy once told a vicar that because of Darwin's book there was no longer any logical reason why the smaller children of oversized families should not be hunted down by sportsmen (*Life*, 321–2; 1904) — a Swiftian joke which earlier welled up portentously into the ultimate Spencerean scene of Little Time's mass murder and suicide, 'Done because we are too menny' (*JO*, 356). Indeed the careers of Time's parental guardians tragically redefine Spencer's dictum that 'Inconvenience, suffering and death, the penalties attached by nature to ignorance, as well as to incompetence — are also the means of remedying these' (*Social Statics*, 1868, 412). It was within this philosophical context that Hardy originally named the novel 'The Simpletons'. Darwin's Malthusian image of nature as battleground, emphasised in Spencer's 'survival of the fittest', proved seminal for Hardy's imagination. A sense of struggle pervades his mature portrayal of relationships, and is classically expressed in the descriptions of the woods around Little Hintock, where the trees are 'wrestling for existence, their branches disfigured with wounds resulting from their mutual rubbings and blows' (*TW*, 339). The struggle is not only sexual but social; it could hardly be otherwise when the author himself was one of those 'strugglers for gentility' whom Mrs Swancourt disparaged in the serial version of *A Pair of Blue Eyes*. Struggle does not necessitate that the world be dominated by cut-throat competition; the dairymaids who are impelled by sexual desire to compete for Angel Clare yield gracefully to Tess's higher claim; when Farfrae's 'fair head' hangs over the window-ledge in his fight with Henchard, the latter draws back in mercy only to be inexorably replaced by the higher degree of economic determinism implicit in the Scot's mechanised business acumen (a scene mirroring the way some animals in the wild spare their defeated enemy so that all healthy males shall mate); Phillotson gives up Sue on sensing the elective affinity between the cousins. Biology provided Hardy with images of competition and of co-operation, and he was careful to quote an *Examiner* article of 1876 which showed how, in the struggle for life, the surviving organism 'is not necessarily that which is absolutely the best in an ideal sense, though it must be that which is most in harmony with surrounding conditions'. Nevertheless it is the ceaseless struggle which begins to predominate in Hardy. The humanely selfless abnegation of a Lady Constantine, or the 'primitive habit of helping one another in time of need' which characterises the Casterbridge populace, become exceptional in a world dominated by predators and victims. When a scientist told Hardy that there was 'an altruism and coalescence between cells as well as an antagonism', the novelist quizzically concluded, 'Well, I can't say' (*Life*, 259; 1893); but he was having his say even as he recorded these remarks, in the composition of *Jude*.

V Adaptation and Specialisation

Evolutionary 'victory', Darwin argued, was gained through adaptability, the qualities accidentally thrown up by genetic exchange which help the creature to fit its environment better and to multiply. Adaptability could mean either specialisation (for example, three different types of mite living off different areas of the honey bee) or generalisation (for example, man, with his widely adaptive capability). Hardy's 'good' characters adapt as beautifully to their environment as Darwin's admired woodpeckers or earthworms; they wrest a living from nature through ingenuity and adaptive creativity. Gabriel Oak, despite vagaries of fortune and weather, is eminently suited to survival, and is described at work in language explicitly resonant of evolution: 'Fitness being the basis of beauty, nobody could have denied that his steady swings and turns in and about the flock had elements of grace' (*FMC*, 48). Similarly Venn, fitting close to the heath, is able to effect the mutation from obsolescent reddle-man to dairy farmer and opportunistically marry Thomasin. The sexual pessimism of later novels means that Winterborne, though similarly adaptable, is not to be saved.

VI Isolation and Invasion

Darwin regarded isolation as a key factor in production of new species on a limited scale. As Hardy read this with regard to his imagined Wessex he saw that isolation would tend to an inbred intensity of emotional interdependence; people so 'insulated' 'get charged with emotive fluid like a Leyden jar with electric' (*TW*, 146). Lines of movement and escape are closed in such a world — as exemplified in Egdon, where the whirlpools of emotion draw the characters ever inward. Darwin also described the invasion of one evolutionary niche by a new species which would oust the previous inhabitants; this is his theory of 'the dominant forms of life' (*The Origin*, 393). Invaders provide the motive force in several places: Maybold, the educated young parson, lightly ruffles the traditional surface in *Under the Greenwood Tree*; Troy, a local of foreign extraction, more powerfully dislocates the common agricultural round, Boldwood's man justly observing that ' "Nothing has prospered in Weatherbury since he came here" ' (*FMC*, 394); in different ways both Fitzpiers, that 'nucleus of advanced ideas' which have 'nothing in common with the life around' (*TW*, 80–1), and Angel Clare carry the contagion of disembodied ideology into Wessex. In *Jude the Obscure* there is no longer any coherent community to be invaded. The most interesting variant of this motif is the career of Clym Yeobright; he is the native termed in African fiction a 'been-to', having visited the metropolitan centre, and he does in effect invade but is reduced by the heath to insignificance. The process is complex: there is a dialectic between the outsider/insider and the natives, so that the reader is not shown simply the invasion of a 'static' rural territory by a dynamic outsider. Such a polarity oversimplifies the structure of feeling in a changing Wessex, a structure given added density by the fact of the author's own role as 'been-to'.

The steady sense of obliteration and replacement of old orders by new is acutely registered in language, the deformation of which expresses the changes in a total culture. Hardy perceives that language is implicated in evolution and social change. Language rests upon an established system which is always evolving, and this truth is crucial in the case of dialect, where the changes will be felt as permanent loss. Although Tess spoke 'two languages' (*TD*, 48) the momentum of change worked against retention of native dialect. Hardy specifically adopted biology as his model in his analysis of dialect, written in 1881, where he speaks of standard English as 'the all-prevailing competitor' against which dialects are 'worsted . . .' in the struggle for existence' (*Prose*, 93). Such linguistic competitiveness, with all its social ramifications, gets dramatised as early as *Under the Greenwood Tree*, where Fancy Day strictly enjoins her father and Tranter Dewy to 'carefully avoid saying "thee" and "thou" in their conversation, on the plea that those ancient words sounded so very humiliating to persons of newer taste' (*UGT*, 204). Hardy took pains in later editions to raise Geoffrey Day's status and conversely to ascribe more dialect forms to Dick in order to emphasise both social boundaries and upward mobility, but Fancy's remark reflects the pressure on women to develop greater sense of status than men and therefore to become more sensitive to the social significance of language variation: whilst women are required to adopt standard forms, men's speech may contain variables which will reflect their masculinity. The exactitude of Hardy's notation could scarcely be bettered. His conclusions on language change are found in his introduction to Barnes's poems, where he ruefully remarks that education has 'gone on with its silent and inevitable effacements, reducing the speech of this country to uniformity, and obliterating every year many a fine old local word' (*Prose*, 76; 1908).

VII   Persistent Types

Although spontaneous change is the rule in evolution, biology also gave evidence of the existence of what Huxley dubbed 'persistent types' — species such as the hatteria which have existed virtually unchanged for hundreds of millions of years by remaining in equilibrium with their environment. Huxley contrasted these creatures with 'dynamic types'. Such a typology affects the relationship between the so-called rustic chorus and the protagonists in Hardy's novels. Darwin argued that 'organisms, considered high in the scale of nature, change more quickly than those that are low' (*The Origin*, 318). Hardy often dramatises this point linguistically, the standard English of his protagonists being exposed in counterpoint to the dialect of the region. Fitzpiers refers to this distinction in evolutionary terms when, gazing at the cider-makers from a hotel window, he tells Grace, ' "I feel as if I belonged to a different species from the people who are working in that yard" '; that this perception is not mere snobbery is confirmed earlier when Creedle tellingly warns Giles to give 'randys' 'only to their own race' (*TW*, 209, 110). The Wessex dialectic between persistent and dynamic types contributes to the sense of simultaneous change and stasis in some of the novels. The heath-dwellers of Edgon participate as more than chorus: they are fundamental to Hardy's intuitive grasp of evolutionary forces as representatives of a type which may survive successive waves of progress unchanged. The novelist was gratified when his evolutionist friend Edward Clodd remarked upon the furze-cutters as 'representing the persistence of the barbaric idea' (*Life*, 230; 1890).

VIII   Organic Interdependence

Evolution is a model not only of change but also of relationship. It implies, rather than a fixed series of 'essences', relationships of like and unlike governed by genetic survival patterns. The meaning of an animal's structure is only comprehended in its relationship with other creatures and with the environment. As Hardy phrased it in 'Drinking Song':

... this strange message Darwin brings. . .
We all are one with creeping things;
  And apes and men
  Blood-brethren,
And likewise reptile forms with stings.

(CP, 906–7)

Hardy is always aware of the interdependent nature of life, and his description of town and country in *The Mayor of Casterbridge* is only the most notable expression of this awareness. *The Origin of Species* dealt substantially with ecology. Darwin explains, for instance, how red clover will flourish in an area where there are many cats to catch mice which would otherwise destroy the nests of humble-bees which are equipped to fertilise the clover (*The Origin*, 125). The intimate and complex manner in which the inhabitants are bound together follows from the fact that all are struggling with finely balanced forces. Such a concatenation is imaged in Darwin's famous description of the tangled bank. Interdependence and process stretch beyond individual creaturely death, as the bodies in the graveyard reappear in 'Transformations' (CP, 472):

So, they are not underground,
But as nerves and veins abound
In the growths of upper air,
And they feel the sun and rain,
And the energy again
That made them what they were!

Huxley had explained the 'continual formation of organic life from inorganic matters' and the equally constant return of 'living bodies to the inorganic world' (*Man's Place*, 159). Evolution thus modifies the Elizabethan conceit of death as expounded in Hamlet's 'A man may fish with the worm that hath eat of a king, and eat of the fish that hath fed of that worm' with a model of energy flowing on a closed circuit of organic and inorganic matter.

More generally Hardy, like George Eliot, perceives an operative network of cause and effect in natural and human orders. Darwin said that 'the several members of each class are connected together by the most complex and radiating lines of affinities' to the extent that it would be impossible to 'disentangle the inextricable web of affinities between the members of any one class' (*The Origin*, 415). Huxley took this further, arguing that 'the higher and more complex the organisation of the social body, the more closely is the life of each member bound up with the life of the whole' (*Collected Essays*, 1894, 125). Hardy transmutes this perception about biological classification systems into the stuff of fiction, projecting an art in which the human race may be shown as 'one great network or tissue which quivers in every part when one point is shaken, like a spider's web if touched' (*Life*, 177; 1886). The human or animal life gains its meaning from a network of differences which define that life. The web of interdependence may enhance the sense of community when the image is used in a conservative organicist way, as it is in the early novels. In the city, connexions may be neither supportive nor perceived, as with the Londoners who 'followed a solitary trail like the inwoven threads which form a banner, and all were equally unconscious of the significant whole they collectively showed forth' (*DR*, 336). In the later novels the 'great web of human doings' (*TW*, 52) stiffens into a chain.

IX   Reversion

Darwin held that domesticated strains could, by growing wild, revert to former aboriginal stock, and that it would not matter if the experiment were to fail (*The Origin* 77). Elements of this notion, blended with the literary treatment of primitivism, fed into the conception of Clym Yeobright, where the reversion to thought and feeling memorialised by community and folklore conflicts with the countervailing impulse to be an educator. The dialectic between the evolving consciousness and its desire to return to communal origins is interestingly muddled here, but more fully articulated in Angel Clare. Given directly sexual connotations reversion was to become a more potent motif for Lawrence.

X Heredity

The design of *The Origin of Species* was to trace lineal descent lines so as to disprove fixity of species. Thus the emphasis of the book fell on heredity and descent, although Darwin was at a loss to account for hereditary processes. The favourite image for the succession of orders, in both Darwin and Haeckel, was that of the tree. Hardy was obsessed by heredity: he constructed his own snobbishly falsified 'Hardy Pedigree', toyed with changing his name to Le Hardy, and remarked upon the 'decline and fall of the Hardys': 'So we go down, down, down' (*Life*, 214–5; 1888). This fiction nourished his secret imaginative life and developed into a myth repeatedly dramatised in the novels, from *A Pair of Blue Eyes*, where Mr Swancourt describes his family as 'coming to nothing for centuries' (*PBE*, 114), through *A Laodicean*, with its fascinated juxtaposition of new and old aristocracy, to the classic treatment of the theme in *Tess*. Darwin wrote that 'the more common forms, in the race for life, will tend to beat and supplant the less common forms' (*The Origin*, 210). Tess, like the de Stancys and others of Hardy's aristocratic remnants, might declare, 'I am merest mimicker and counterfeit' ('The Pedigree', *CP*, 460–1), sharing as she does with Jude and Sue 'a doom or curse of hereditary temperament' (*Life*, 271; 1895). The genealogical concerns of Hardy and some of his characters echo those of Darwin, since the naturalist remarked on the difficulty of showing 'blood-relationship between the numerous kindred of any ancient and noble family' and deplored the absence of 'pedigrees or armorial bearings' in nature (*The Origin*, 413, 457). Spencer had likewise noticed that in 'the picture-galleries of old families, and on the monumental brasses in the adjacent churches, are often seen types of feature that are still, from time to time, repeated in members of these families' (*Principles of Biology*, I, 252). Towards the end of his career as a novelist Hardy read Weismann's *Essays upon Heredity* of 1889, which distinguished between the individual body, the 'soma', not concerned in reproduction, and the hereditary constitution contained in 'germ-cells'. This theory conferred upon humanity a kind of vicarious immortality:

I am the family face;
Flesh perishes, I live on,
Projecting trait and trace
Through time to times anon,
And leaping from place to place
Over oblivion.

The years-heired features that can
In curve and voice and eye
Despise the human span
Of durance — that is I;
The eternal thing in man,
That heeds no call to die.

('Heredity', *CP*, 434)

That Weismann's theory, neatly expressed in this lyric, would yield diminishing returns on a larger scale is evidenced by the triviality of *The Well-Beloved*. More intimately, Hardy shows a sense of style as inherited. By gradually discarding his showy citational mannerisms he absorbs and transforms his models, appropriating literature and art to his special purpose and marrying them to intimate folk memory. In his own writing practice as a novelist he formally embodies the evolutionary paradox of heredity as conservative force interacting with the revolutionary possibilities of variation.

XI   Sexual Selection

With the exception of *The Mayor of Casterbridge* sexual matters are at the nub of every Hardy novel. Whilst his handling of relationships intimately reflects the pattern of his own infatuations and disillusionments, the reading of Darwin helped to structure these real or imaginary experiences into fiction. The theory of sexual selection, seen by Darwin as an adjunct to natural selection, but by Wallace as largely a question of mimicry and protective colouring, provides a Darwinian iconography for Hardy's courtships and marriages. Darwin argued that sexual differentiation, dimorphism, arose as a result of reproductive advantage, and that in order to seize such advantages males would develop two complementary sets of characteristics: weapons (for example, antlers in deer) with which to fight for the chosen female (now read as fights over territory); and attractants, such as colourful coats, plumage, scent and so on. Darwin held that females in nature exerted choice, and this is perhaps borne out by the fact that they necessarily expend more energy than the male in the reproductive process. Display qualities would be marked where there was a surplus of males or where polygamy was the norm: Manston, Troy, Wildeve, Fitzpiers, d'Urberville and Pierston are all polygamous by nature. In his curious 'conversion' d'Urberville temporarily adopts the dark protective colouring of a ranter, a kind of mimicry hastily abandoned on sight of Tess, who conversely adapts to anonymous field woman by shaving her eyebrows and wearing dun-coloured clothes. The creation of Diggory Venn owes much to the thesis of protective colouring; and in such episodes as Mrs Charmond's seizure of Marty's hair for the purpose of sexual allure, and Arabella's hair-piece, Hardy makes neat play with mimicry. Sex, as nature says in one of Hardy's poems, is biologically a 'lure that my species/May gather and gain' ('The Mother Mourns', *CP*, 112), and the function of sexual selection is performed through the range of modes of epigamic selection: in the first the male is stationary and attracts the female through call and song (as in many bird species); in the second the female is stationary and attracts the male (as in some species of moth); in the third both sexes are mobile (as in butterfly species). Lines of sexual rivalry and courtship procedures delineated in the new biology constituted a potent model for the novelist. Whilst male rivalry was a commonplace of the Victorian plot, the revelation of sexual selection made available a whole range of modulations and variants upon which Hardy's sensibilities worked powerfully. As early as *Far from the Madding Crowd* he made Oak cry out biblically against 'the woman whose heart is snares and nets' (*FMC*, 183), and elsewhere he sententiously designated as woman's 'ruling passion' the wish 'to fascinate and influence those more powerful than she' (*PBE*, 218). A fundamentally passive man, it is likely that Hardy saw himself as lured into a mutually destructive marriage (indeed, the second Mrs Hardy told a friend that Hardy had been trapped into matrimony by the machinations of Emma's sister). At the height of the Hardy's marital crisis in the nineties the novelist plangently remarked, 'it has never struck me that the spider is invariably male and the fly invariably female' (*The New Review*, June 1894, 681). The sexual conjunctions and disjunctions were suggestively outlined by Huxley:

there are organic beings, which operate as *opponents*, and there are organic beings which operate as *helpers* to any given organic creature. The opponents may be of two kinds: there are the *indirect opponents*, which are what we may call *rivals*; and there are the *direct opponents*, those which strive to destroy the creature; and these we call *enemies*.

(*Man's Place*, 236)

Thus the aesthetic of Hardy's novels may be related to the formalist notion that narrative plots reduce themselves to a range of finite possibilities and that characters are classifiable into 'nouns' such as hero, villain, despatcher, helper, donor and so on, and that the action may be reduced to the structural relationship of subject versus object, sender versus receiver, or prohibition versus violation. Biology gave Hardy the analogy for human behaviour he was seeking, as may clearly be seen when the relationships are tabulated.

Females	Males
DR: Cytherea Graye, in rivalry with Adelaide Hinton for Springrove	Edward Springrove, Aeneas Manston; rivalry here culminates in a fight; note how Manston flatters himself that the interest Miss Ald-

clyffe takes in him was propelled 'by the same law of natural selection' which makes him attractive to females 'en masse' (*DR*, 191)

UGT: Fancy Day

Dick Dewy, Mr Shiner, Mr Maybold

PBE: Elfride Swancourt

Felix Jethway (from the grave), Stephen Smith, Henry Knight, Lord Luxellian

FMC: Bathsheba Everdene, in rivalry with Fanny Robin for Troy

Gabriel Oak, Sgt Troy, Mr Boldwood

HE: Ethelberta Petherwin, in rivalry with her sister Picotee for Julian

Christopher Julian, Eustace Ladywell, Alfred Neigh, Lord Mountclere

RN: Eustacia, in rivalry with Thomasin for Wildeve

Clym Yeobright, Damon Wildeve

TM: Anne Garland

John Loveday, Bob Loveday, Festus Derriman

AL: Paula Power; Charlotte de Stancy is an undeclared rival for Somerset, but retreats to an Anglican sisterhood

George Somerset, Capt de Stancy

TT: Viviette Constantine

Swithin St Cleeve, Bishop Helmsdale; a variant in which one man's child is 'fathered' on the other

MC: Lucetta Templeman, in rivalry with Eliabeth-Jane for Farfrae

Henchard, Farfrae ('the supplanter', MC, 222); 'the sense of occult rivalry in suitorship was so much superadded to the palpable rivalry of their business lives' (*ibid.*, 207)

TW: Grace Melbury, Felise Charmond in rivalry for Fitzpiers; Marty South a silent rival for Winterborne

Winterborne, Fitzpiers; Mrs Charmond tells Grace, ' "Man-traps are of rather ominous significance where a person of our sex lives, are they not?" ' (TW, 89)

TD: Tess Durbeyfield, in rivalry with the milkmaids for Clare, and with Car Darch for d'Urberville

Alec d'Urberville, Angel Clare

WB: Avice Caro, Avice the younger, Avice the third, Marcia Bencomb

Pierston

JO: Sue Bridehead, in rivalry with Arabella Donn for Jude

Jude Fawley, Phillotson

A *table of sexual rivalry in Hardy's novels*
'the call seldom produces the comer, the man to love rarely coincides with the hour for loving. Nature does not often say "See!" to her poor creature at a time when seeing can lead to happy doing' (TD, 72); 'As the male is the searcher, he has required and gained more eager passions than the female' (Darwin to Wallace, 1868)

Such a table has a schematic look, but the density of the situations and ideas about sex, resulting in misalliances, passion, guilt, regret, and so forth leaves the simplicity of the biological model far behind. One variable motif, for instance, is Hardy's occasional toying with the idea of mating a lower-class male with an upper-class female to produce more vigorous stock and to rise socially in accordance with the formula expounded by Stephen Smith's mother that 'men all move up a stage by marriage' and 'mate a stage higher' (*PBE*, 123). However much this owes to Hardy's childhood fantasies about Julia Augusta Martin it derives its compulsion from biological theories of vigour obtained through crossing — an idea current at the time (cf. Strindberg's *Miss Julie* of 1888, with its 'split and vacillating' characters), and always likely to crop up in Hardy from 'The Poor Man and the Lady' onwards.

There is fascinating contrast in the novels between the gradual social progress of formal courtship and naked display scenes in which sexual selection as theory gets transformed into symbolic action. The discourse of courtship gives place to the image of selection. This accounts for a series of remarkable Darwinian scenes in the novels when 'the male of his species' (*HE*, 219) sheds the demands of etiquette. Showing rather than telling is already fully realised in the texture of *Desperate Remedies*, when Cytherea takes refuge in the storm and is impelled to listen to Manston playing the organ. The use of music as sexual attractant — this is Manston's 'call' to her — is underlined in the language, which describes how the sounds 'shook and bent her to themselves' so as to invade her with 'new impulses of thought' which lead her to 'involuntarily' shrink closer to the man under stress of storm and sound. Recovering her balance she regrets having been 'excited and dragged into frankness by the wiles of a stranger' (*DR*, 167–8). As the narrator reflects later, Cytherea's interest is in Manston's 'marvellous beauty' which renders him like 'some fascinating panther or leopard' (*ibid.*, 172), a man 'whose presence fascinated her into involuntariness of bearing' (*ibid.*, 262). That involuntariness recurs with Hardy's women right up to the seduction of Tess, and provides the donnée of 'The Romantic Adventures of a Milkmaid'. Manston, Miss Ald-

clyffe's illegitimate son, re-enacts towards Cytherea the role
his father had played towards the elder Cytherea; in the
American edition of 1874 Miss Aldclyffe referred to herself as
a young girl 'decoyed into a secret marriage' (*ibid.*, 435). The
Manston–Cytherea tableau is the most outstanding of several
passages where *Desperate Remedies* abandons the compulsive
readerliness of the sensation novel which the audience pas-
sively consumes, and moves towards a participatory exhilara-
tion. These rewarding moments of climactic intermittence
grow in the later works where bourgeois conventions of
realism are increasingly challenged, rules of internal consis-
tency discarded, and contextual appropriateness undermined,
the metaphorical tableaux blocking and diverting the
metonymy of plot-line. Music as sexual attractant, neatly
handled in Maggie's reaction to Stephen Guest in *The Mill on
the Floss*, recurs in Hardy in Elfride's piano-playing to Stephen
Smith, or with greater subtlety of erotic suggestion in 'The
Fiddler of the Reels'. In *Far from the Madding Crowd* Hardy
daringly manipulates sexual selection into a tableau of erotic
feeling. Darwin had observed how, in some species of birds,
'males display their gorgeous plumage and perform strange
antics before the females, which standing by as spectators, at
last choose the most attractive partner' (*The Origin*, 137).
Hardy suspends the narrative flow to dramatise a sexual
transaction of just this type in the scene entitled, 'The Hollow
amid the Ferns', where Troy's sword-play encircles the passive
figure of the woman:

In an instant the atmosphere was transformed to Bathsheba's eyes. Beams of
light caught from the low sun's rays, above, around, in front of her,
well-nigh shut out earth and heaven — all emitted in the marvellous
evolutions of Troy's reflecting blade, which seemed everywhere at once, and
yet nowhere specially. These circling gleams were accompanied by a keen
rush that was almost a whistling — also springing from all sides of her at
once. In short, she was enclosed in a firmament of light, and of sharp hisses,
resembling a sky-full of meteors close at hand.

Hardy foregrounds the sweeping movement which engulfs the
human figure; little wonder that at the close of the episode

Bathsheba 'felt powerless to withstand or deny him' (*FMC*, 216–18): many of the heroines exhibit a similar will-less passivity at critical moments. Hardy expertly projects the non-linguistic codes which pertain in sexual matters in animal and human worlds so that the scene feels like a projection of the unconscious in which the figure of the male dissolves into a swaying tension. Discursive content is nil. Hardy responded to Stephen's editorial demand that Troy's seductive qualities be treated 'in a gingerly fashion' by creating a presentational symbolism which retains its untranslatability in the tension with a plot of which the reader needs to make sense. The tableau, a characteristic blend of poetic, erotic and absurd elements, mimetically renders a complex of motive, desire and feeling which amply justify the author's brooding over scientific evidence. Hardy's art fuses together Mill's definition of science, which 'acts by presenting a proposition to the understanding', and of poetry, which offers 'interesting objects of contemplation to the sensibilities'. The courtship encounter which provides the staple of nineteenth-century fiction is defamiliarised here as it is in the first meeting of the two, with its odd sense of the invasion of one self by another through language which declares its bold sexuality:

'Are you a woman?'
'Yes.'
'A lady, I should have said.'
'It doesn't matter.'
'I am a man.'
'Oh!'

(*ibid*., 192–3)

In the novel Troy's role as Darwinian displaying agent is contrasted with Oak's as patient: 'Troy's deformities lay deep down from a woman's vision, whilst his embellishments were upon the very surface, thus contrasting with the homely Oak, whose defects were patent to the blindest, and whose virtues were as metals in a mine' (*ibid*., 220).

There are other such scenes, in which spoken language gives places to interpersonal communication derived from biology, for instance Paula Power's gymnastic display or Farfrae's Scottish singing and dancing, but one striking instance of 'the margin of the unexpressed' in Hardy's texture will suffice — Angel Clare's harp-playing at Talbothays Dairy, which lures Tess 'like a fascinated bird' (*TD*, 161):

> The outskirt of the garden in which Tess found herself had been left uncultivated for some years, and was now damp and rank with juicy grass which sent up mists of pollen at a touch; and with tall blooming weeds emitting offensive smells — weeds whose red and yellow and purple hues formed a polychrome as dazzling as that of cultivated flowers. She went stealthily as a cat through this profusion of growth, gathering cuckoo-spittle on her skirts, cracking snails that were underfoot, staining her hands with thistle-milk and slug-slime, and rubbing off upon her naked arms sticky blights which, though snow-white on the apple-tree trunks, made madder stains on her skin; thus she drew quite near to Clare, still unobserved of him . . . she undulated upon the thin notes of the second-hand harp. . . . Though near nightfall, the rank-smelling weed-flowers glowed as if they would not close for intentness, and the waves of colour mixed with the waves of sound.
>
> (*TD*, 161–2)

This is a passage of unresolved complexities; syntactically it loops together strings of dependent clauses which enact Tess's trance-like movement through the garden, a place redolent with traces and gleanings from *Hamlet* and the Bible, and yet transformed into a uniquely Hardyesque tableau in its presentation of the attraction/repulsion of the plants and the near synesthesia of the last sentence. The transference of feeling is skilfully managed, and the simile fails to disturb, indeed supports, the overall reduction of Tess to the plant world, then her hypnotic approach and dance-like movements which are mimed by the reading mind's stumbling through the dense syntax. The pleasurable insidiousness of hypnosis is hinted at in this undulating movement. The supplanting of garden flowers by somewhat exotic weeds hints both at the deracinating effect of Clare's intellection upon an agricultural community and at Tess's 'idolatry' of him, which is 'too rank, too wild, too deadly' (*ibid.*, 256). The quality of Clare's ethical position is registered by the second-hand harp. This fine mesh of detail yields up image rather than statement, but it is an image which defines the developing relationship. The scene is aptly illustrative of epistemic choice: the writer's consciousness exploring the rich confusions inherent in the human relevance of the new scientific theory. As often in Hardy the language appears to be following one pattern whilst the reader's imagination is engaged by undertones or contrary patterns, the meanings stated or implied tugging creatively in various directions. If literary sources serve to give allegorical depth the theory of sexual selection provides the underlying motivation. Hardy was right to claim that his art was 'to intensify the expression of things' (*Life*, 177; 1886): the intensification here plays upon epigamic selection to body forth the dramatisation of wordless sexual attraction. Human perception and feeling shifts beyond subjective control in such expressive scenes to be transformed into an 'outer' universe which may reflect, distort or threaten the individual's reaction. Man's place in nature will vary in accordance with mood and artistic perspective. The feeling in the garden-scene is for the thing itself, rather than as in some of Hardy's weaker scenes for the act of feeling. In this writing, with its projection, sensuousness and moral ambiguity, Hardy intuitively reaches what Conrad named 'the secret springs of the responsive emotions'.

XII Extinction

Evolution is not necessarily upwards to higher levels. There are periods of stagnation and efflorescence (for example, the origination of flowering plants 150 million years ago led to an explosion of insect species so that they now comprise three-quarters of all species). Fast rates of evolution (as in reaction to pesticides, industrial melanism in moths and butterflies, or resistance to DDT) may alternate with slow rates, stagnation or eventual extinction. The geological evidence Lyell gave of the extinction of orders was vital to Darwin's insight that species were not fixed. While Hardy rarely envisages radical extinction (though one or two of the poems dwell on the prospect of a dead earth) the personal extinction of so many of his protagonists takes some of its tincture from evolution and from his biased reading of heredity which enabled him to melodramatise his own role as 'the last one' of his line ('Sine Prole', *CP*, 721), or of the d'Urbervilles, 'extinct — as a county family' (*TD*, 36). In adapting patterns of species elimination to the human level Hardy overthrows the dominant liberal tradition of the Victorian novel which acts on the assumption that whatever tragedy befell the individual the tendency of human relationships was ameliorative. The Christian charity which informs Hardy's ethical code ceases, in the late novels, to be a guide to effective survival conduct. Whilst Maggie Tulliver's death is local, Jude Fawley's, possessing a typicality achieved through 'sensuous generalisation of the whole man', stands as evidence of the coming universal wish not to life discerned by a novelist who characterised himself as coming 'of an old family of spent social energies' (*Life*, 5).

Knight's ordeal on the cliff in *A Pair of Blue Eyes* shows the young writer already pondering extinction and survival of the fittest. Clinging to the cliff face 'in the presence of a personalised loneliness', Knight senses the 'inveterate antagonism of these black precipices to all strugglers for life' — he is forced to participate actively in the Darwinian drama which he knows (as he knows everything) intellectually. He finds himself staring at a fossilised trilobite, an early crustacean order which Darwin and Huxley had pointed out as an instance of relatively sudden extinction through failure to adapt. The strata speak to Knight of the immensity of geological time in which the higher consciousness of man was a recent development. As he is a 'fair geologist' his mind drifts back to the aeons before man:

Huge elephantine forms, the mastodon, the hippopotamus, the tapir, antelopes of monstrous size, the megatherium, and the myledon — all, for the moment, in juxtaposition. Further back, and overlapped by these, were perched huge-billed birds and swinish creatures as large as horses. Still more shadowy were the sinister crocodilian outlines —alligators and other uncouth shapes, culminating in the colossal lizard, the iguanodon. Folded behind were dragon forms and clouds of flying reptiles:

The scene is double-dyed in ambiguity: whilst the rain pours down Elfride strips off her underclothing so that her dress 'seemed to cling to her like a glove', and with the rope thus formed she pulls Knight to safety. As they embrace she watches a steam-boat passing which carries in it Knight's now extinguished rival and erstwhile pupil, Stephen Smith. Yet the pair do not kiss: 'Knight's peculiarity of nature was such that it would not allow him to take advantage of the unguarded and passionate avowal she had tacitly made' (*PBE*, 238–46). The scene, clumsily executed and tonally disparate, anticipates Hardy's mature art in its sense of a power the reader is at a loss to account for. It is permeated with the author's understanding of evolution: Knight's consciousness has refined itself beyond the point where he can act decisively in emotional matters (like his two models, Horace Moule and Thomas Hardy). He is faced with extinction, but saved by Elfride's ready adaptability. Her act is a sexual declaration which Knight's fastidious neurosis about 'purity' will not allow him to take up. Knight knows he has a good brain, and thinks that it would be 'loss to earth of good material' if he fails, and that 'some less developed life' should be taken. He does not learn the lesson of the trilobite, and his dreams of a prehistoric earth may prompt recall of Freud's note that 'with neurotics it is as though we were in a prehistoric landscape'. Knight is the most interesting figure in the book, and looks forward to other portraits of neurotics – notably Angel Clare and Sue Bridehead — characters in whom the evolved intellect has led to hypersensitive ethical indecision, division of the self into 'higher' and 'lower' and consequent mistrust of the 'frail casket' of the body (*ibid*., 288). Knight cannot change until it is too late, and he and Smith mourn impotently over Elfride's coffin. But her death is no more than fictional contrivance: it is Knight who wills his own extinction in the struggle for a mate. He lacks the extrovert virility (such are the satires of circumstance) of the 'fossilised Tory', Mr Swancourt. The scene, prophetically conceived in the light of Moule's suicide a year later, obtrudes into the lighter texture of the surrounding chapters a dissonant node of ideas, desires and conflicting images peculiar to

Hardy's imaginative assimilation of evolutionary thought; the central uncertainty is to be located in Hardy's own doubt as to how he should present his odd hero.

No such uncertainty mars the polarity of change and extinction in *Tess*. When Tess's 'rally' from her seduction is thwarted by Angel Clare's discovery of her secret, she is subjected to a period of agricultural hardship which prefigures her execution at the hands of society. Schooled to patience she works upon the 'starve-acre' land of Flintcomb-Ash grubbing up and slicing swedes in bitter winter conditions. In this activity the girls are reduced to 'mechanical regularity' of movement, wage-slaves who try to blot out the drenching rain by dreaming of summer in the Froom valley. Their only visitants are the 'strange birds from behind the North Pole' who have witnessed 'scenes of cataclysmal horror' in the polar regions, visitants from a region of white obliteration such as that depicted in Friedrich's arctic painting, 'The Wreck of the Hope' (*TD*, 331–4). The winter suffering is followed in March by the episode of the steam-threshing machine, 'the engine which was to act as the *primum mobile* of this little world' as Spencer's First Cause did to the universe, replacing a beneficent creator as implacably as the absentee landlord of Flintcomb-Ash destroys the feudal agricultural community. Obedient to the ministrations of the sooty operative with the 'strange northern accent', the machine inexorably reduces the farm-labourers to exhausted automata serving the cause of blind process. The irruption of Alec, whose money was made through usury, and Tess's act in repelling him with the bloody blow on the mouth, bodies out the implications of the arrival of the machine. Marx claimed that under capitalism the worker 'is a mere machine for producing foreign wealth, broken in body and brutalised in mind', and Hardy here mobilises, absorbs and transforms the scientific materialism and commercialism of his time into a scene which juxtaposes natural-organic (universe as tree) with mechanical (universe as machine — what Carlyle termed the 'huge, dead, immeasurable Steam-Engine'). The culmination of *Tess* thus has its roots in a deeply-felt clash between romantic and evolutionary versions of reality. Coleridge held that objects were 'essentially fixed and dead' whilst imagination was 'essentially vital'; for Blake 'Art is the Tree of Life' whilst 'Science is the Tree of Death'. The suffering and exploitation of Tess and her fellow-labourers on the rick, their own subsequent cruelty to the cornered rats, Tess's belated honeymoon with Angel Clare, and her arrest and execution act out the confusions of moral purpose to which evolution had unwittingly given rise. Huxley himself, in his 1893 Romanes lectures, spoke of the confusion attendant upon mixing up the terms 'fittest' and 'best', and argued that no ethical principles could properly be founded upon processes of random survival. The practice of that which is ethically 'best' 'involves a course of conduct which, in all respects, is opposed to that which leads to success in the cosmic struggle for existence'. Ethics were intended to modify, rather than reproduce, natural processes, since the only good guaranteed by evolution is the survival of whatever makes for survival. The dehumanising mechanism which re-orders the rhythms of the countryside at Flintcomb-Ash acts as a metaphor for the iron law of evolution; yet the coming together of Liza-Lu and Angel Clare in the final paragraph hints at the self-renewal available to evolutionary process.

Hardy accompanied his poem 'Nature's Questioning' with the sketch of a broken key in a lock. That emblem sums up his position, which insists upon the unknowability of the universe and man's bafflement at his role — part victim, part agent — within the process. George Eliot remarked that the Darwinian thesis produced in her a 'feeble impression compared with the mystery that lies under the processes'. Whilst he was struck by the 'mechanic artistry' of nature revealed in evolution theory ('To a Motherless Child', *CP*, 66), Hardy would have concurred. 'Nature is played out as a Beauty', he observed in 1887, 'but not as a Mystery' (*Life*, 185). Understanding of evolution alleviated neither economic distress in Wessex nor private anguish at Max Gate. It stood nonetheless in his mind for enlightenment and progress, 'the sure, unhasting, steady stress/Of Reason's movement' ('A Cathedral Facade at Mid-night', *CP*, 703), and after the Great War Hardy commented grimly that 'belief in witches of Endor' was 'displacing the Darwinian theory and "the truth that shall make you free" ' (*Prose*, 57; 1922). Whatever aspects of struggle Darwin had revealed in nature, the most profound insistence of his argument was upon the unity in diversity of living things, on the corporeality man shares with other organisms, and on recognition of a universe which imposes limits on human self-will. Hardy endorsed these concepts, and expressed them variously in novels which speak of man and environment co-existing in one complex process. It was a vision rendered with all the intensity at his command, and the tragic novels record a radical extension of moral sympathy. Within the 'universal concert of things' man, with all other creatures, forms part of the life of the universe. Man's bodily life, his heredity, his emotions, and his evolving consciousness belong within the general scope of nature: no bifurcation can be made between soul, organism and environment. Hardy justly sum-med up himself in 1909: 'The discovery of the law of evolution, which revealed that all organic creatures are of one family, shifted the centre of altruism from humanity to the whole conscious world collectively' (*Life*, 346).

2 *The Spencerean Native*

Hardy's creative misreading of Darwin contributed to the creation of a private mythology, the projection of the Hardy psychology into the external world, which underpins the novels. The psychic evidence of his early courtships, ruinous first marriage and later flirtations needs to be linked in the critical estimate with his prolonged grappling with the implications of the new science. The novelist who made notes on Leslie Stephen's thesis that Darwinism would prove fruitful in its sociological application (*Literary Notes*, 137; 1880) would necessarily extend that application to his own reading of man and society. Engagement with evolutionary thinking determined the peculiar formal properties of Hardy's novels, generated as they are out of implicit scientific theory and private obsession. Each new work aptly registered the nineteenth-century concept of time as continuous motion which could only be comprehended in its trend away from an original cause. The process of becoming related to the future of each protagonist in a world dominated by genetic process through which cause engendered effect, but the time-scale differed between novels: Henchard's wife-sale is the primum mobile of his tragedy, worked out in a single lifetime, whereas Tess's disposition and career issue from Durbeyfield prehistory. The characters move or more often blunder forwards through time but the significance of their actions is to be comprehended backwards. Evolution provided a metonymic base for a writer of Hardy's allusive metaphoric turn of mind, and what he denigrated as the 'unconsciously paralyzing influence' of censorship (*Letters* II, 90; 1895) proved crucially beneficial to his imaginative bent towards expressive projection. The notebooks reveal him turning over the consequences of evolution for man, looking at biology from a variety of angles; but the ground-bass of these ruminations, as he noted from J.A. Symonds, was that man be treated 'as part of the natural order' (*ibid.*, 67; 1876), a being 'entirely subordinate to the World — each living being to its own environment', as Comte had asserted (*ibid.*, 76; 1876). Whether Hardy is prepared to go beyond this level of causation towards an acceptance of G.H. Lewes's claim that all mental processes were '*functions* of physical processes' (*ibid.*, 95; 1877) is debatable. What is clear is that Hardy's expressionism both endorses and undercuts the scientific hegemony of evolution by dramatising and 'picturing' the clash between subjective and objective views of the phenomenal world. Hardy's style, that is to say, is his idiosyncratic way of inhabiting the new world of scientific materialism.

The complexity of the dialectic between Hardy and evolutionary doctrine is especially manifest in his reaction to the works of Herbert Spencer he is known to have read — *First Principles* (1862), the *Essays* (1865), and *Principles of Biology* (1865–7). Spencer might have claimed, like Los in *Jerusalem*, 'I must create a System or be enslav'd by another Man's'. His evolutionary system-building, adumbrated in *First Principles*, issued in the massive project of the Synthetic System. Edward Clodd asserted that Spencer had dealt with the whole sweep of evolution 'from gas to genius', but Darwin privately remarked that Spencer's deductive generalisations had 'not been of any use'. Whereas Darwin accounts for the genesis of natural kinds through adaptation, Spencer's system accounts for life on the basis of the continuous redistribution of matter and motion. *First Principles*, a crucial work for Hardy, defines evolution as 'a change from a less coherent form to a more coherent form, consequent on the dissipation of motion and integration of matter' (*First Principles*, 262), or again as a change from 'an indefinite, incoherent homogeneity, to a definite coherent heterogeneity' (*ibid.*, 307). In man this individuating process is marked by 'struggles for supremacy' which must 'finally be decided in favour of some class or some one' (*ibid.*, 343), both individual and society developing at different rates of change. The motor for evolution in Spencerean metaphysics is the persistence of force, which reflects an 'Ultimate Reality' called 'the Unknowable'; the mechanism is a mélange of natural selection and adaptation, and Lamarckian inheritance of acquired characteristics; the process is the metamorphic change undergone by all species. If force is dissipated in action it must be reconstituted in reaction; this is what Spencer designates 'rhythm'. Spencer gives as the reasoning behind his sociology the evolutionary belief that society displays phenomena ascribable to the character of its units and to the conditions under which they exist. He passes, without any sense of an illicit jump, from describing the behaviour of single inanimate objects to 'aggregates of men' and thence to society — his positivist upbringing compelling him to apply organic laws to society. The system is riddled with contradictions: because the transmission of environmentally-induced traits to the next generation is what happens in culture, Spencer clings to it in biology; he fails to distinguish between development of the embryo, which is genetically determined, and evolution of the species, which is not; and he is forced to argue that character, shaped by inheritance, shapes institutions, and also conversely that institutions shape character.

Spencer's intellectual edifice resonated with the experience of those to whom it was addressed. The synthetic system was truly systematic only in its demonstration of truth through rhetoric, but it acted as a kind of dynamic fiction within the culture which produced it. This scientifically oriented vision was of absorbing interest to Hardy during the years of his intellectual formation, when *First Principles* acted, he recalled, 'as a sort of patent expander when I had been particularly narrowed down by the events of life'. In the same letter of 1893 he conceded, 'Whether the theories are true or false, their effect upon the imagination is unquestionable' (*Letters* II, 24–5). The shape of Hardy's later novels is congruent with the synthetic system, tracing out large movements of evolution and dissolution. The imprecision of Spencer's thought, its orotundities and verbiage, mattered less for his original readers than the insights into agencies of human and social change. Incorporation of speculative philosophy into the life of the imagination was essential artistic strategy for Hardy, whose whole habit of understanding formed itself out of his reading and experience in the eighteen-sixties. Behind the exaggeration and coincidence of the novels there is a sense of the pressures of the new thought being translated into the experience of men and women in isolated rural communities. Shifts of sensibility accompany changes in the material base in *The Woodlanders, Tess* and *Jude the Obscure*, but they also throw up modulations of personal anxiety and psychic discomfort. Tess, never alien to herself or environment, is alienated by male versions of her. In Jude's character the collision between Alec and Angel is internalised and interwoven with the educational theme. Such contradictions as Angel, Jude or Sue embody have prior existence in the mind of the writer, and make manifest the disjunctions co-existent in his consciousness between a private peasant idiom and articulate public speech. No feat of adaptation in the novels is more spectacular than that of their author's leaping across class barriers driven by ambitions of self-help whilst yet retaining to the end the unstable vitality of his studiously masked class origins. The impact of *First Principles* is not simply upon the level of ideology but of art: in the eighteen-sixties Spencer contributed seminally to the formation of that proprietary consciousness so typical of Hardy's narratives. The imprint of Spencer may be traced in several aspects of Hardy's fiction, but crucially in structure and characterisation.

Spencer held that life consists of 'an extremely complex kind of movement', a movement which 'begins, rises to its climax, declines, and ceases in death'. Each individual 'exhibits a wave of that peculiar activity', so that during longer epochs 'whole orders have thus arisen, culminated, and dwindled away' (*First Principles*, 209–10). The history of anything must 'include its appearance out of the imperceptible and its disappearance into the imperceptible' (*ibid.*, 222), the origin of the imperceptible being ascribed to that mysterious First Cause which Sue believes 'worked automatically like a

somnambulist' (*JO*, 362). In Spencerean terms the evolution
of life is defined as the tendency towards individuation: 'in
becoming more distinct from each other, and from their
environment, organisms acquire more marked individualities'
(*Principles of Biology* I, 150). The process is marked by
increasing organisational complexity as the web of modifying
causes achieves 'an intricacy that is scarcely conceivable'
(*ibid*., 418). Spencerean evolution denominates the arch-form
as the aesthetic patterning of experience; things, Hardy
reflects, 'move in cycles' (*Prose*, 126; 1890), but the movement
is out of the imperceptible, into differentiation, and back
again. Hardy observed that one of the most imposing features
of the 'human mass' was its 'passivity' (*Notebooks*, 6; 1870),
and the aesthetic ordering of his novels increasingly takes the
Spencerean form of life emerging from, then lapsing back into,
homogeneous darkness. In Hardy's phraseology this represents the movement from nescience to sentience to nescience.
Such a simplistic wave-like motion scarcely does justice to the
dynamics of the novels, but Spencer's vision of life underlines
the tragic drift of the later books. Spencer required a principle
to show how order was maintained, and uncovered this in the
equilibrium between force and matter, arguing that when
complete equilibration was reached, evolution would end.

Hardy's work records an increasingly complex sense of
human personality; the wholehearted simplicity of a Gabriel
Oak gives way to characters whose outlines are shifting and
tentative. Beginning with Knight, Hardy became aware of the
tragic implications of evolution — separation from environment and self-division wrought by higher consciousness. In the
aesthetic plan of the novels Hardy defines a widening gap
between his 'universal' man and contingent social reality. The
wholeness of community typified by the Mellstock Quire is
subsequently splintered into a conception of heroes and
heroines which divided them from the secondary people.
Protagonists are torn between real and ideal, and devote their
energies to reconciling these irreconcilable domains; secondary characters are conformist and integrated into a social

world from which they profit. Such splitting is complex; the exceptional individual is evolving away from his roots, and there is an external gap between man and landscape, but this divorce is also internalised into inner conflict — Angel Clare, Jude and Sue are only the most extreme victims/agents of a tendency already explored in the experiences of Clym Yeobright. The disjunction of thought from instinct, mind from body, is outlined by Spencer, who predicts a 'progressing differentiation from the environment' of the higher forms (*Principles of Biology* I, 144) marked by an organism's 'greater unlikeness' to its surroundings (*ibid.*, 148). This results in the contrast between dynamic and passive types which marks the drama on Egdon, in the Hintock woods, or at Talbothays: 'The more highly developed the organism becomes, the stronger grows the contrast between its activity and the inertness of the objects amid which it moves' (*ibid.*, 149). Although Spencer recognised that human evolution presupposed 'higher nervous development and greater expenditure in nervous action' (*ibid.*, II, 502), his positivist creed enabled him to affirm that such evolution would tend towards 'an increasing amount of happiness' (*ibid.*, I, 354). Hardy, though deeply imbued with these writings, felt otherwise: division of labour and separation of classes alienate man not only from nature but from himself.

In 1888 Hardy projected a 'sensation' novel which would differ from its type in that 'the sensationalism is not casualty, but evolution'; not, that is to say, 'physical but psychical' (*Life*, 204). Such a work was already written, in *The Return of the Native*, with its Spencerean ground-plan. The germ-theme of the novel lies, not in Egdon, but in the presentation of Clym, and especially in the delineation of the 'typical countenance of the future' (*RN*, 191). The beauty of the Yeobright physiognomy will soon be 'ruthlessly overrun by its parasite, thought', a 'disease of the flesh' which 'bore evidence that ideal physical beauty is incompatible with emotional development and a full recognition of the coil of things' (*ibid.*, 162). Clym's portrait explores further the implications of the characterisation of

Knight, the sense that dissatisfaction with civilised existence or a narrow mode of inner life can become so radical as to demand a different alternative whilst at the same time recognising that this need is itself the result of civilised habits of self-analysis. The pessimism of heightened self-consciousness in Clym owes something to the Arnoldian examination of Hellenic and Judaic thought-patterns, but it is crucially evolutionary. The bodying out of Clym and later tragic individuals endorses Huxley's prognostication that 'subtle refinement of emotion' is 'fatally attended by a proportional enlargement of the capacity for suffering' (*Collected Essays*, 1893–4, IX, 55). The cost, to both Clym and his creator, of psychic evolution, is debated in the sub-text of *The Return*, in the countervailing movements of heath/metropolis, civilisation/primitivism, light/darkness, activity/passiveness, which underpin the readerly requirements of the plot. Spencer's 'higher nervous development and greater expenditure in nervous action' lie at the root of the contradictory tendencies within Clym. The hero feels alienated by the process of individuation, and simultaneously attempts two contradictory modes of resolving the contradictions which will otherwise destroy him: on the one hand he envisages an educational programme through which 'bucolic placidity' will quicken to 'intellectual aims' (*RN*, 196); on the other he attempts to sink back into the life of the heath, 'a mere parasite', 'fretting its surface in his daily labour' and 'having no knowledge of anything in the world but fern, furze, heath, lichens, and moss' (*ibid*., 297). Hardy recorded de Laveleye's thesis that 'in the social order, as in Nature, all must change slowly, and by evolution' (*Literary Notes*, 156; 1883), and the forced and unnatural mode of Clym's idealism is comically announced in the hair-cutting scene. That scene concludes, not with Clym's resounding rhetoric, but with the countryman's verdict that the young man ought to 'mind his business', a remark which distils the complex divisions between dynamic and static, primitive and civilised, in the novel: what *is* Clym's 'business'?

The line of demarcation is neatly imaged in the types of bonfire visible from the heath, conflagrations which reach back to primitive fire-festivals, purging the forces inimical to growth and, imitative of the sun, guaranteeing its continuance. Whereas the 'great ones had perished', other fires 'small in magnitude beside the transient blazes' prove more enduring (*RN*, 56). The heath-dwellers, with their bonfires, mumming, maypole and pagan customs, outlast the heroic protagonists like Eustacia, who feels that a 'blaze of love, and extinction, was better than a lantern glimmer' (*ibid.*, 96). When she first appears silhouetted against the sky the narrator portentously remarks that she is 'more likely to have a history worth knowing' than the peasants preparing the bonfire (*ibid.*, 42). The opposite proves to be true, and Hardy's socially ingenuous artistic preference for over-refined sensibility to working-class mores and what Spencer termed 'aboriginal conceptions of good and evil spirits' (*Principles of Biology* I, 334) shows up glaringly in the 'Queen of Night' chapter, and in the general sense of contrast between a heroine who, by virtue of her shadowily improvised foreign background is déclassé, and the firmly-hinged (if mechanically conceived) lives of the furze-cutting fraternity. Hardy said that any community would contain a small minority of 'sensitive souls', and that these were the individuals 'worth observing'. His self-interested commitment to rising gentility reinforces this distinction between the 'mentally unquickened' and the 'living, throbbing, suffering, vital' (*Life*, 185–6; 1887). Indeed the fissures in the map of Clym's personality, fractured between maternal ambition, socialist idealism and self-abnegation, derive primarily from the self-division of his creator. Whilst Clym develops into a case-history of the ache of modernism, Eustacia and Wildeve do little to disturb readership expectations for their *Belgravia* or subscription library audience. Their hot-and-cold affair, and the mistreatment of Thomasin, constitutes what Fairway calls the 'great racketing vagary' of the central action, an action which relates too nakedly to a melodramatic Ur-text. Whilst the transformation of Eustacia from witchcraft to Bovarysme may be felt to count as a gain in verisimilitude, Hardy's imaginative attention is elsewhere, primarily in the treatment of Clym and his mother, and in the relation between evolving dramatic types and the primitives of Egdon.

That the evolving graph of such a novel is not simple is borne out by an analysis of the dialogue, in which minutiae of social differentiation are signalled. Hardy's acute ear enabled him to grasp intuitively the way sentence structure and vocabulary range indicate social class, and he was specially alive to tensions between language which represented a permanent socio-economic group and that which had a shifting communicative role. Reality is a viewpoint determined by the place of the character in the class structure, and Hardy's close awareness of the structure of consciousness of his characters tends to alter the very style of his novels. In *The Return of the Native* there is an increase in the interaction of social conventions over previous novels, both in the author's expressive deployment of the cultural conventions encoded in language and in the demands made upon the reader in releasing meaning from such deployment. There is no straight polarisation between dialect and non-dialect speakers, but rather a mixed sense of the non-evolved charms of dialect forms and the class insistence of reader and writer that only standard speakers are capable of tragedy. Hardy said his aim was to convey 'the spirit of intelligent peasant talk' (*Prose*, 91; 1878), and the social homogeneity and paganism of the furze-cutting group are accordingly rendered in proverbially dense dialectal speech made suitably legible for a middle-class audience. The heroic protagonists necessarily speak in standard forms, but the most interesting area is the language of those neither 'evolved' nor 'primitive', notably Diggory Venn and Mrs Yeobright, whose language varies according to the auditor. Venn, compelled by the exigencies of the plot to vacillate between weird outsider and respectable citizen, is capable of wide variations of tone and vocabulary. When chatting to Johnny Nunsuch the reddleman draws on such locutions as 'Who be ye', 'Beest hurt', 'fainty', ''tis grow'd into my skin' and so on; in the next scene, with Eustacia, he speaks deferentially in standard form: 'I have made so bold, miss, as to step across and tell you some strange news'. The reddleman rose uncertainly in the social scale in the manuscript, serial and first edition, and the linguistic imprecision relates primarily to Hardy's inability to transform peasant into capitalist farmer without a sense of incongruity — in the first book edition, Diggory even acquired a bank balance. Language mobility here reflects the Egdon social spectrum, and those characters occupying the middle ground reveal how Hardy struggled with his own sense of communal history and personal evolution. Mrs Yeobright, as the daughter of a curate, adopts standard forms, but the pressure of common speech informs her talk and serves to accentuate the social ambition channelled so fiercely into her well-spoken son. Such class-oriented distinctions arise in the inner ear of a novelist who embodied his mother's social pretensions, who kept his snobbish wife well away from his more bucolic relations, and yet remained personally close to his 'broad' brother Henry.

Whilst Mrs Yeobright deplores Clym's return to Egdon, elsewhere that return is diagnosed as a force which will awaken and fertilise the intransigent heath. Eustacia feels his influence 'penetrating her like summer sun' (*RN*, 149), and the sexual and natural co-exist in Hardy's studied seasonal plan, and in 'The Fascination', when the heath awakens from a 'winter trance' into a 'flowering period' which coincides with the onset of passion (*ibid*., 213, 261). Cyclic presentation had been commonplace since the Middle Ages; what renders it different in *The Return* is the underpinning of Hardy's evolutionary reading beneath the seasonal love drama. In his study of Huxley, Clodd maintained that 'even the highest faculties of feeling and intellect begin to germinate in lower forms of life'. The heightened self-consciousness of Clym, his desire for completion and social fulfilment, originate in that primal world which his mother glimpses in the muddy pool 'amid which the maggoty shapes of innumerable obscure creatures could be indistinctly seen, heaving and wallowing with enjoyment' (*ibid.*, 297). The Victorian reader might have found it a shorter step from these joyful ephemerons to Christian Cantle than from the peasants to Clym. Certainly the opening description is at pains to portray a world of homogeneous gloom marked by 'apparent repose of incredible slowness' (*ibid.*, 40). Only gradually does life — the decayed captain, the reddleman, Eustacia and the peasants silhouetted against the sky — emerge in what is a precise fictional rendition of Spencer's movement from homogeneity to heterogeneous differentiation. What is termed in one chapter heading 'The Inevitable Movement Onwards' dictates the course of the action — from inertia into life, and back to inertia. Even in this drama of emergent life, Hardy differentiates between the peasants, with their tools, co-operation and socially defined speech, and the romantic protagonist with her inward thought and passion, set against the organising social unit.

After the deaths of the children in *Jude the Obscure* the doctor, an 'advanced' man who has doubtless read his Spencer, pronounces it 'the beginning of the coming universal wish not to live' (*JO*, 356). The tendency towards annihilation in the late Hardy novels, the 'silent bleed of a world decaying' ('Going and Staying', *CP*, 573), has been generally remarked. Whilst it is a tendency arising from a multitude of causes, artistic and psychological, it markedly echoes a basic tenet of Spencer's theory, the principles of dissolution about which *First Principles* is especially eloqent. Dissolution, 'the absorption of motion and concomitant distintegration of matter' (*First Principles*, 228), means that the ultimate end of evolution lies in 'omnipresent death' (*ibid.*, 413), and the Spencerean rhetoric of a universe in which 'all is sinking/To dissolubility' ('Genetrix Laesa', *CP*, 771) became deeply attractive to Hardy as he mulled over the idea in his final novels. Whilst the deaths of Elfride or Troy serve the exigencies of plot, the deaths of Winterborne, Henchard, Tess and Jude ramify into statements about the world in which they lived, about the pain and separation inherent in change, and about a universe in which energy seems to be running down and 'Normal unawareness waits rebirth' ('The Aërolite', *CP*, 770) — the whole process of Spencer's 'universal death' (*First Principles*, 423). Indeed, the most severely architectonic structure, in *Jude*, serves to contain the most extreme anarchies of feeling and disintegration.

The running down of organic process is marked less obviously in the increasing silence of the major characters. Speech can ultimately never pierce the profound silence of subjective thought in which each person is the whole world to himself. Through language man admits others into his own singularity in order to create meaningful discourse; language, as Marx said, is in this sense the direct reality of thought. But the possibilities for meaning grow less and the silence deeper in the late novels, as they did between the couple in Max Gate. This explains the inarticulate loves of Winterborne and Marty, emotion locked within the socialised and inhibited 'personality'. Darwin had demonstrated how creatures, in order to survive, needed to interpret a complex referential system of signals. To do this a range of paralanguages such as sound, appearance, colour and gesture required decoding. In considering man, the 'language animal', Huxley observed that nothing in natural selection was able to account for human speech. Articulation of meaning is necessary to life; the end of life in an evolved universe will also be the end of speech and meaning. Language, existing at a certain level of abstraction and universality, presupposes a social contract between its users. But because it is a convention about signs it may fail to convey intricacies of feeling, and the human being may split in two, the one having the experience, the other expressing this complex of feeling in conventionally received terms. Sue Bridehead feels this split most acutely. In *Tess* and *Jude* the society-forming functions of literature may be detected; these works of literary imagination help to determine the idea of society which is their prerequisite, a society in crisis moving towards final dissolution. Silence comes to mean more than language to Jude and Sue, 'one person split in two' as Phillotson calls them (*JO*, 250), so that they are able to communicate beyond words in a 'second silent conversation' (*ibid.*, 224). Earlier, Mrs Yeobright and her son, 'the right and the left hands of the same body' (*RN*, 212), find that 'words were as the rusty implements of a bygone barbarous epoch' (*ibid.*, 218), a discovery that results in the mother's final descent into silence and death on the heath and conversely in the son's wordy exhortations to the heath-dwellers. There is in such relationships a sense of what cannot be spoken inhering in what is said.

The movement of Hardy's tragic novels is not simply towards death; he also explores the principle of psychic inertia whereby tensions are reduced to a minimal level by the mind acting as though it could lower itself to a state of extinction. In this drive for inertia and release the process of repetition represents the effort of the mind to restore a state which is historically primitive and marked by a draining away of energy. It is thus with Clym as furze-cutter: his 'return' takes the form of immolation to the heath in what Eustacia derides as 'shameful labour' — the repetition, the 'monotony of his occupation' (*ibid.*, 274–5) acting to bring about a primal psychic inertia which returns both him and his environment to prehistory:

The air was warm with a vaporous warmth, and the stillness was unbroken. Lizards, grasshoppers, and ants were the only living things to be beheld. The scene seemed to belong to the ancient world of the carboniferous period, when the forms of plants were few, and of the fern kind; when there was neither bud nor blossom, nothing but a monotonous extent of leafage, amid which no bird sang.

(*ibid.*, 227)

The Keatsian echo here serves to emphasise the sinking back into silence which preludes the mental and physical dissolution Clym fearfully desires in the 'oppressive horizontality' of Egdon (*ibid.*, 230). In each tragic novel the 'unsympathetic First Cause' (*TD*, 195) works towards this end: Henchard on the heath, Tess on the scaffold, Winterborne out in the woods,

Jude on his death-bed. Clym, like Joseph Arch, is viewed by his creator as a 'social evolutionist' (*Prose*, 184; 1883), but his ineffectual idea of progressive enlightenment has to struggle with the countervailing movement towards dissolution on 'obsolete' Edgon (*RN*, 198), a movement which Hardy's sense of aesthetic fitness demands. Discounting the compromise ending and concentrating on the 'austere' version Hardy refers to in his footnote enables the reader to trace out the pattern of Spencerean evolution. Characters participate in the atmosphere of dissolution: from the reddleman, a 'nearly perished link between obsolete forms of life and those which generally prevail' (*ibid.*, 38), through Wildeve, brought down from engineering to inn-keeping and anticipating a yet 'lower stage' (*ibid.*, 90), to Eustacia herself, whose figure first stands above Rainbarrow like 'a sort of last man among them, musing for a moment before dropping into eternal night with the rest of his race' (*ibid.*, 41). The manifestations of life running down in the characters are mirrored in nature, for example in the arrival from the north pole of birds possessing 'an amplitude of Northern knowledge' of 'Glacial catastrophes, snow-storm episodes, glittering auroral effects' (*ibid.*, 113). Such creatures, whom Spencer had described 'driven by stress of weather from the remote north' (*First Principles*, 363), would reappear at Flintcomb-Ash with dire foreboding. Clym predicts a time when he and Eustacia will both say, ' "I have attained my faith and purpose" and die' (*RN*, 222), and in the first edition vows to keep his wife and mother apart 'till the universe come to an end'. Clym undergoes diminution of sight and ambition to experience a type of psychic death, whilst the other protagonists, his mother, wife and rival lose organic force and life. The death of the lovers on a night when the sky was 'closed up by cloud and rain to the degree of extinction' effects a final 'harmony' between the 'chaos' of mind and the external world (*ibid.*, 370–7), a harmony desiderated in Hardy's fiction by his adherence to Spencer's law of the persistence of force. Spencer had postulated external forces tending to bring living bodies 'into that stable equilibrium shown by inorganic bodies', and

internal forces 'by which this tendency is constantly antagon-
ised'; maintenance of this antagonism was more fundamental
than 'the unceasing changes which constitute life' (*First
Principles*, 60). Unceasing change affects the characters in
both feeling and ideology: the superstitious world of Susan
Nunsuch is giving place to Yeobright's Comtean enlightenment. Yet this process may also register as a sense of loss and
alienation, a transfer from the Egdon world in which 'the
several parts constitute a co-operative assemblage' (*ibid.*, 263)
to the denatured world of advanced thought. The differences
between Yeobright and the rustics 'once commenced must
tend to become ever more marked' (*ibid.*, 343). These
differences are embodied in the implied comparison between
communal anonymity in the mumming play, with its easy
pliability, and the dependence on written symbols which leads
Clym towards a myopia both physiological and social. It was
with reference to the 'subterranean world' of oral tradition
that Hardy exclaimed to Clodd, 'how vast and striking is the
body of unwritten human experience in this so-called literary
age' (*Letters* II, 202; 1898). These are differences rooted in
conceptions of time which remain totally at variance: the
communal world of the rustics is one which returns to its
sources in a continual round of festivals, celebrations and
ancient practices which, like the maypole dance, render
publicly their concept of time as circular, a circularity inherent
in the repetition of oral tradition, in an enclosed landscape like
Egdon, and in the seasons. Clym imports into Egdon the
linearity of modern literary consciousness, a straight-line
rationalism which posits man as a being still making himself
and the world around him.

The novelistic action is determined at the deepest level by
unresolved antagonisms between corrupting idealism, male
and female, natural and metropolitan, environment and
culture. It is a final ironic stroke that it is the superficial
Wildeve and the undefined Eustacia who achieve romantic
apotheosis through death. But Eustacia has merely separated
herself from the heath; Clym, higher in the scale of evolution,

suffers more acutely: the process of individuation results in the more damaging separation from self, and it is just that the novel should end with his lonely figure. He will never marry or procreate. Spencer wrote that 'every higher degree of individual evolution is followed by a lower degree of race-multiplication' (*Principles of Biology* II, 410), and the childless author visits this barren fate on most of his advanced thinkers. When Jude and Sue overturn Spencer's dictum the consequences are predictably awful. Both victim and agent of evolution, in the language of his open-air sermons Clym Yeobright embodies that fatal split of the modern self in its search for wholeness and authenticity. The narrator observes that Clym speaks 'not only in simple language on Rainbarrow', 'but in a more cultivated strain elsewhere' (*RN*, 423); but everywhere to an audience largely impervious to his message.

The process of dissolution dramatised in the increasing alienation and sense of catastrophe of the later Hardy novels may be conceived under the Spencerean shadow, therefore. Yet there is always running counter to even the bleakest moments a sense of enduring values in work and love, a fuller definition of self attained whatever the odds. The structure of feeling in Henchard, Tess or Jude is complexly founded in oral tradition, community of work, social solidarity, set against the evolution necessitated through increased personal and class mobility. The middle-aged Thomas Hardy remained creatively vulnerable to the manifold presences of family and social history.

3   Forster: Nature and Nurture

Forster's *Maurice* was a secretive contribution to the debate
about man's place in the evolutionary scheme. Its tendency is
to assert man's creative individuality against a society ordered,
regimented and ratified by the rationalist world-view. *Maurice*
made art out of abstraction, and what is achieved in the work
is best defined against its ideological background. Forster's
terminal note of 1960 provides the context. The story was the
result of a visit to Edward Carpenter at Milthrope, a visit to a
sage whom the novelist approached 'as one approaches a
saviour'. The plan of the novel, with its three characters and
happy ending, 'rushed' into Forster's pen when Carpenter's
companion touched the novelist on the backside (*M*, 217).
Forster returned to his mother 'in a state of exaltation, feeling
that the fog had cleared from his life' and began work on the
story (*Life* I, 257). This was in September 1913, but Forster's
interest in Carpenter dated from around 1907, when he seems
to have done the bulk of his reading of the socialist pioneer. In
addition to the prose poem *Towards Democracy* (1883), a
work in which Forster discerned Carpenter's 'love for the
individual and for the beauty of nature', by the time of
composing *Maurice* the novelist also knew *Civilisation, Its
Cause and Cure* (1889), *Love's Coming of Age* (1896), *Angels'
Wings* (1898), *The Art of Creation* (1904) and *The Intermediate Sex* (1908).

Forster judged Carpenter 'a remarkable fellow, lovable,
charming, energetic, courageous, possibly great' (*Two Cheers*,
205–7), and after his visit kept in touch with the Milthorpe
community. The Whitmanesque ethos of natural joy and
fellowship espoused by Carpenter attracted Forster at a time
of personal crisis, and he later consulted Milthorpe about his
affair with an Alexandrian tram-conductor. The loneliness
followed by fulfilment experienced in Alexandria echoes

events in the novel Forster had completed two years earlier: when Maurice is abandoned by Clive, Forster points out that 'he was doing a fine thing—proving on how little the soul can exist' (*M*, 127). A period of barrenness prepares the way for sexual fulfilment in the manner prescribed by Carpenter: 'Remain stedfast, knowing that each prisoner has to endure in patience till the season of his liberation; when the love comes which is for you it will turn the lock easily and loose your chains' (*Towards Democracy*, 352). One method of attaining this degree of steadfastness, endorsed by both writers, was through the sublimation of social work. Carpenter writes of an upper-class woman building up her girls' club and of a young man organising 'his boys from the slums', adding that 'something more, more personal and close, than philanthropy inspires them' (*ibid.*, 401). The something more is frankly sexual in Forster; having described Maurice's work with boys in south London he observes that 'Certain obscurities of the last six months became clear. For example, a pupil at the Settlement — He wrinkled his nose, as one who needs no further proof' (*M*, 132). *Maurice* was thus conceived as a Carpenterian novel of sexual freedom and pantheist aspiration, and may be read in conjunction with a diary entry which Forster made at the end of 1913 after completing the book:

year has ended with 3 months of exaltation and India has made me more of a 'personage'— more able to defend my sterility against criticism, less swayed by the speaker of the moment. I think this is all. Forward rather than back.
   Edward Carpenter! Edward Carpenter! Edward Carpenter!
                                                                    (*Life* I, 258)

At the time of the composition of *Maurice* Forster was also mulling over the ideas of Samuel Butler. He was reading *Life and Habit* (1878), a work which, 'with its praise of instinct as the basis of right conduct, lent a kind of support to Carpenter's teaching' (*ibid.*, 258). In the autumn of 1914 Forster even planned to write a study of Butler. Thus this 'master of the oblique' was in the forefront of Forster's thought at the time. Like Carpenter, Butler possessed a special significance for Forster, although the latter considered himself to have 'a more poetical mind'. He allowed Mr Emerson to quote Butler's essays in *A Room with a View*, a borrowing which signals the mutual interests: Italy, music, relations between money and culture, and the issues of evolution, mating and survival treated in *Life and Habit*. The thesis of *Life and Habit* is that Darwin's explanation of evolution was unsatisfactory: he had not accounted for the variations on which natural selection worked. In the five editions of *The Origin of Species* published after 1859 Darwin modified his theory, and after scrutinising all editions Butler felt ready to expose logical difficulties inherent in Darwinian theory. He felt that Darwin's thesis was too random, and by emphasising the agency of mind he reintroduced an element of teleology into nature. Butler believed that an organism's inheritable habits induce organic changes and give the creature a purposive evolution. Darwin had not proved that natural selection was the origin of species, but rather had utilised it as a deux ex machina, and so his argument was inherently circular — any species which survived had done so because of natural selection. The theory could be stretched to fit all cases and was fundamentally untestable. Butler preferred to insist that unconscious memory held the key: the identities of parents and offspring were continuous and stretched back to primordial beginnings. The analogy of memory and heredity was attractive to Lamarckians until the rediscovery of Mendel. The acquisition of character, it was held, is like learning; since characters so acquired are inherited in proportion to the intensity of the producing stimuli, inheritance is like memory. Learning is retained through memory, which is enhanced by constant repetition. Thus acts invoked at first by conscious thought become automatic through repetition. In this argument instinct is unconscious remembrance of things learnt so powerfully that the germ-cells are affected and pass on the trait to future generations. If behaviour can be learned then inherited as instinct, morphological features may be acquired and inherited in a similar way. Ontogeny in this view is the organism's memory of its past history: 'The small, structureless, impregnate ovum from which we have each one of us sprung, has a partial recollection of all that has happened to each one of its ancestors prior to the period at which any such ancestor has issued from the bodies of its progenitors' (*Life and Habit*, 297). The heritable nature of memory is Butler's major premise: memory becomes instinctive knowledge acquired through the conscious effort of past generations. The individual is one with and part of his progenitor, his 'past selves' live in him, since parent and germ-cell are linked in a continuous chain, in which each individual never dies. With the force of memory and accumulated experience a variation could not persist. Butler presupposes a type of intelligence inventing or choosing new habits and structures, and losing consciousness of its efforts once the habit is learnt to perfection. Self-conscious knowledge is as nothing compared with unconscious memory. The better we know a thing the less conscious we are that we know it, and only those things performed without consciousness are perfectly known. Butler includes willing with knowing and defines two categories of acts: those which must be learnt (for example, eating), and those which are innate (for example, swallowing). Man has least control over 'acts' like digestion which he shares with his invertebrate ancestors. Butler tries to verify this thesis by arguing that unborn creatures show uncanny knowledge of what they want and how to get it — for example, the chick tapping at the egg shell. According to this argument each individual derives its identity from the primordial cell. The infertility of hybrids emphasised by Darwin is ascribed to divergent parental memories handed on to the embryo by its parents. Blind chance in the universe is reduced by a modified Lamarckism: creatures may make an effort to respond to felt needs and acquire necessary habits which they transmit to their offspring as unconscious memories. Butler considers that what counts towards 'successful' species is that they:

were capable of feeling needs, and that they differed in their needs and manner of gratifying them, and that they continued to live in successive generations, rather than the fact that when lucky and wise they thrived and bred more descendants.
                                                              (*Life and Habit*, 265)

Variation arises in a creature 'through a sense of its needs' and 'through the opening up of new desires in many creatures'. Such variants will 'depend greatly on differences of individuality and temperament' — the very differences that Maurice and his creator struggle with in the novel (*ibid.*, 267). As habits form they become instincts so that 'consciousness of knowledge vanishes on the knowledge becoming perfect' (*ibid.*, 17).

Relaxation into a new norm of instinctual behaviour tallies with much in Carpenter and is a norm which Forster proposes in his fiction. Butler's conclusion is that 'instinct, in the great majority of cases, is habit pure and simple' (*ibid.*, 221). If this is so there can be no clear-cut moral distinction between one instinct and another: sexually, Forster must have felt, the instinct for male love was as justifiable as the heterosexuality canonised by religion and law. Open acknowledgement of such love, with consequent changes in social and private behaviour, would be an instance of variation opening up new survival patterns. Evolution, though still determinist, becomes more acceptable to the liberal humanist in its Lamarckian form. 'There is a force at work throughout creation', Carpenter held, 'ever urging each type onward into . . . newer forms', a force which appeared first 'in the form of desire' (*Civilisation*, 175). Forster was plagued at this time by the pressure of his own unacceptable desire, whilst incapable of the hedonist abandon of Bloomsbury. The notions of Carpenter and Butler fed in to the conception of *Maurice*, in which Forster objectifies, dramatises and releases some of the pressures. The novel finally rejects even Butler's modified determinism in favour of Carpenter's individualism, and its conclusion may represent an evasion of the full implications of evolutionary thought. Evolution frets the surface of Forster's earlier novels; in *The Longest Journey* Stephen, an otherwise model Carpenter hero, reads avidly in the third-rate literature of the subject, 'Darwin, minus the modesty'. But it is in *Maurice* that these issues are focussed. The ideological clash between Carpenter and Butler derives from romantic theory, with its dual design upon nature of, first, losing individual consciousness in an ecstatic blending with the cosmos whilst, secondly, categorising natural phenomena with rigorous precision. *Towards Democracy* and *Life and Habit* are both generated by the 'new' nature of romanticism, and Forster fleshes out the contradictions in *Maurice*.

The theme of the book is predicated in its opening scene at the seaside between Maurice and his prep school master Mr Ducie. Ducie, rationalist in outlook and 'soaked in evolution', draws diagrams of the sexual organs in the sand and analyses intercourse 'scientifically and sympathetically' — a pseudo-humanitarian venture Forster acidly dismisses as useless since manhood must steal upon the boy 'in a trance'. The futility of the attempt, and Ducie's conformity, are neatly registered by the master's panic when, looking back at the sands he recalls the diagrams and sees a mixed party approaching them. He runs back 'sweating with fear' only to witness the tide obliterate all trace of his barren rationalism. Maurice learns that Ducie is despicable, and then 'darkness rolled up again, the darkness that is primeval but not eternal, and yields to its own painful dawn' (*M*, 19–20). The lines of movement in the novel are adumbrated here: rationalist evolutionary thought, with its stress on mating and survival, matched against a freer concept of nature and instinct. It is no accident that Ducie reappears to be decisively defeated at the climactic interview between Maurice and Scudder in the British Museum, nor that Maurice irritably rejects Lecky's *History of Rationalism* as appropriate reading-matter at the crisis of his sexual anxiety. Ducie's evolution reduces man to mechanical insignificance in a cosmic process inaccessible to man's understanding, an inhumane scientific overview in which humanity dwindles to what Butler called 'parts and processes of life at large' (*Life and Habit*, 124). Forster challenges this, and insists on the centrality and otherness of people. It is significantly Clive Durham, after conversion to sexual 'normality', who thinks along conventional evolutionary lines, that 'Not only in sex, but in all things men have moved blindly, have evolved out of slime to dissolve into it when this accident of consequences is over' (*M*, 104). Man's insignificance in the general design comforts Clive's sense of nullity, but Forster's sympathies are engaged elsewhere. Clive, the parasitism of his class position made manifest in the incipient decay of the estate, attempts mutation from private landowner to man of affairs with his attempt to enter parliament. Whilst his good-humoured egotism masks this change from homosexual to heterosexual, private to public man, Clive's transformation represents a last throw of the evolutionary dice. Although he may not deny the ubiquity of evolution, Forster modifies and humanises the ethical brutality of its social-Darwinist application. After Clive's change the novelist comments, 'It was nothing to [Maurice] that Nature had caught up this dropped stitch in order to continue her pattern' (*ibid.*, 120). The holiness of the heart's affections, the primacy of individual suffering and joy, are insisted upon by Forster against the empirical reordering of experience by inevitable process. In some aspects nature itself is felt as perverse, the normative function stressed in *The Longest Journey* and *Howards End* queried at places in the narrative. Such moments work primarily as metaphorical projection of inner misery upon outer scene, but in the realisation of the Wiltshire estate Forster ruminates upon Hardy's Unfulfilled Intention:

Blossom after blossom crept past them, draggled by the ungenial year: some had cankered, others would never unfold: here and there beauty triumphed, but desperately, flickering in a world of gloom. Maurice looked into one after another, and though he did not care for flowers the failure irritated him. Scarcely anything was perfect. On one spray every flower was lopsided, the next swarmed with caterpillars, or bulged with galls. The indifference of nature! And her incompetence!

(*ibid.*, 156)

The language aptly mirrors and creates a mind at the end of its tether, but there is more here than pathetic fallacy: emotion completes sense-perception. For Forster, man is the answer, and the social-Darwinist ploy of transferring observations from animal to human worlds is exposed to an unflagging humanist critique. At Cambridge, for instance, Maurice is surprised to find that life does not consist of continuous struggle. He was 'only waiting for such an atmosphere himself to soften. He did not enjoy being cruel and rude. It was against his nature. But it was necessary at school, or he might have gone under, and he had supposed it would have been even more necessary on the larger battlefield of the university' (*ibid.*, 31). Nurture distorts nature into a battleground where only the strong survive; Forster had already examined the notion in Sawston School. The battleground Darwin discerned in the natural world is not the last word on human or natural life. The Spencerean formula of survival is weighed against a more romantic version of pastoral.

Forster's novel explicitly takes issue with biology in the matter of marriage and children. Exclusively homosexual life must preclude these central human relations. *Maurice* is a Carpenterian story of homosexual fulfilment which triumphs in rejecting the family. Early in the novel the choric figure of Dr Barry announces the received wisdom that 'Man that is born of woman must go with woman if the human race is to continue' (*ibid.*, 30). The nexus of ideas is aired in an exchange between Clive and Maurice. When Clive reflects on the need of an heir for Penge, his country estate, Maurice is prompted into unwonted thoughts of mortality and sterility:

An immense sadness — he believed himself beyond such irritants — had risen up in his soul. He and the beloved would vanish utterly — would continue neither in Heaven nor on Earth. They had won past the conventions, but Nature still faced them, saying with even voice, 'Very well, you are thus; I blame none of my children. But you must go the way of all sterility.' The thought that he was sterile weighed on the young man with a sudden shame. His mother or Mrs Durham might lack mind or heart, but they had done visible work; they had handed on the torch their sons would tread out.

He had not meant to trouble Clive, but out it all came as soon as they lay down in the fern. Clive did not agree. 'Why children?' he asked. 'Why always children? For love to end where it begins is far more beautiful, and Nature knows it.'

(*ibid.*, 90)

That conversation is echoed parodistically by the second pair of male lovers:

'I hear everything you say,' said Maurice thoughtfully, and continued in exactly the same tone: 'Scudder, why do you think it's "natural" to care both for women and men? You wrote so in your letter. It isn't natural for me. I have really got to think that "natural" only means oneself.'

The man seemed interested. 'Couldn't you get a kid of your own, then?' he asked, roughening.

'I've been to two doctors about it. Neither were any good.'

'So you can't?'

'No, I can't.'

'Want one?' he asked, as if hostile.

'It's not much use wanting.'

'I could marry tomorrow if I like,' he bragged.

(*ibid*., 194)

Forster's mastery of the material enables him to blend the elements finely here; definition and redefinition of the key-word 'natural' and its implied extension to incorporate Alec's coarser-grained character is subtly linked with science's blinkered ideological attempts to interfere with that nature, the verbal nuances held in balance between the elaborated and restricted codes of Maurice and Alec. This scene in the museum between Alec, Maurice and Ducie provides the opportunity for crisis, revealing traits in each man which expose his prime typicality. Social and emotional worlds are bound together persuasively in the text, the destinies of the individuals growing out of, and beyond, contingent reality. The question of offspring is the crux of the evolutionary problem in Forster, and one with which he could only tinker in *The Longest Journey* or *Howards End*. Children in Forster remain ciphers, emblems of continuity like the children of Stephen Wonham or Leonard Bast. Forster's shying away from the issue, his wish to stress heredity without handling its mechanics, is revealed in *The Longest Journey* by Mr Failing's glimpse of a naked boy on the roof of Cadover. After her husband's death Mrs Failing finds among his papers a sentence which puzzles her: 'I see the respectable mansion. I see the smug fortress of culture. The doors are shut. But on the roof the children go dancing for ever' (Ch. 12). *Maurice* marks a turning-point: for the first time Forster rejects marriage and dispenses with the need to have children dancing in the fictional wings. It was an intractable problem which he shared with his intellectual mentors. Butler had written in his notebooks, 'Bodily offspring I do not leave, but mental offspring I do', and Carpenter held that the 'other', homosexual love, 'has its special function in social and heroic work, and in the generations of those children of the mind, the philosophical conceptions which transform our lives and those of society' (*The Intermediate Sex*, 70). The defiance in each case is shrill, but this was inevitable having regard to the sexual situation. Forster picks up the theme in *Maurice*, and airs it again in *A Passage to India* where he ultimately fudges the issue by having Fielding marry Stella Moore. A conversation earlier in the novel revealed a different sub-text:

> 'I don't care for children.'
> 'Caring has nothing to do with it,' [Aziz] said impatiently.
> 'I don't feel their absence, I don't want them weeping around my death-bed and being polite about me afterwards, which I believe is the general notion. I'd far rather leave a thought behind me than a child. Other people can have children.'
>
> (Ch. 11)

There is discomfort here, signalled by the death-bed image which obtrudes a Victorian trope into a recognisably modern impasse, and by the faked opposition between children and ideas, but Forster is honestly seeking an alternative to the 'tragedy of the bedroom' which dominates the realist novel and which attains its apotheosis when Sue opens Phillotson's door at the end of *Jude the Obscure*. It was part of a complex situation for Forster, and he sought in the action of his secret novel to rebel against the marriage tradition of his earlier, public work, and to endorse Havelock Ellis's warning about seeking to 'destroy also those children of the spirit which possess sometimes a greater worth than the children of the flesh'. *Maurice* is generated from Carpenter's premise that 'the prime object of Sex is *union*, the physical union is the allegory and expression of the real union, and that generation is a secondary object or result of this union' (*Love's Coming of Age*, 28–9). Carpenter predicted a revolution 'in peoples' views of the place and purpose of the non-childbearing love' (*The Intermediate Sex*, 115–16), and in a talk on Whitman argued that the 'continuation of the race' was less significant than 'consolidation of a new form of life'.

Popular objection to this view might centre on the sterility to which Forster referred in his 1913 diary entry. This was a topic which had been dealt with by Butler in relation to hybridisation. Forster may have weighed his words and applied them to the disintegration of the relationship between Clive and Maurice:

this sterility has nothing to do with any supposed immutable or fixed limits of species, but results simply from the same principle which prevents old friends, no matter how intimate in youth, from returning to their old intimacy after a lapse of years, during which they have been subjected to widely different influences, inasmuch as they will each have contracted new habits, and have got into new ways, which they do not like now to alter.

(*Life and Habit*, 180)

Forster had to come to terms with sterility for himself and his fictional protagonist, whereas Butler was able to imagine that man is truly immortal, since each individual is '*actually* the primordial cell which never died nor dies, but has differentiated itself into the life of the world' (*ibid.*, 86). Forster broke through this barrier in 'Little Imber', written in 1961, where the desire for progeny issues in the fantasy fulfilment of male 'wrestling' producing a new strain of babies to alleviate female sterility, the production of 'Romuloids and Remoids in masses' (*Arctic Summer*, 235), whereby 'males had won'. Butler had, however, dealt with the creative possibilities opened up by cross-breeding and hybridisation; again Forster may be seen introducing this into the body of the novel. Cross-breeding, Butler argued, was a beneficial 'irritating stimulant' which prevents man from passing through life 'as though in slumber' (*Life and Habit*, 29). All species 'are occasionally benefited by a cross; but we should also expect that a cross should have a tendency to introduce a disturbing element' (*ibid.*, 173–4). The elements of disturbance and the invigorating effects of crossing both registered upon Forster's imagination and helped counter his fears of homosexual sterility. He frequently made the transition from cross-breeding as biological phenomenon to the mixing of social and class groups. Cross-breeding dominates the plots of both *The Longest Journey*, in which Stephen Wonham is the vigorous product of the union of two classes, and of *Howards End*, in the Bast-Helen affair. In *Maurice* it is introduced conventionally in the linking of the two families, the aristocratic Durhams and the bourgeois Halls. When Mrs Durham is 'looking out wives for Clive' she 'put down the Hall girls on her list'. 'She had a theory', Forster writes, that 'one ought to cross breeds a bit' (*M*, 92) — a sly echo of his current reading. Cross-breeding is treated more ambitiously in the developments between Maurice and Alec, whose relationship enacts Carpenter's panacea for social ills: 'The only road back to sanity is through the re-mingling of classes and masses, and the large readoption of the modes of life, thought and speech still current among the latter.' Sexual love was 'a sentiment which easily passes the bounds of class and caste' (*The Intermediate Sex*, 115–16).

Forster emphasised that it was in Sheffield that Carpenter found 'the people who suited him: artisans, unemployed, toughs, it is to them that his heart went out' (*Two Cheers*, 205). This circles round Forster's own predilections: the men who 'suited' the novelist were preponderantly working-class. By attaching himself to such vigorous stock, and through the homosexual choice of self in the guise of a virile alter ego, Maurice emerges from the depression ensuing from Clive's return to normality. He is resurrected and delivered into a life of sexual fellowship in the woods. The narrative moves from realism to romance, but gains poetic substance through its engagement with the nexus of ideas propounded by Carpenter and Butler. The final move is predicted in a rejection of the proprieties when Maurice refuses to acknowledge royalty because they live 'inside a ring fence' (*M*, 187), a judgement which reformulates Carpenter's condemnation of the 'stuffiness and narrowness' of bourgeois marriage when the couple live surrounded by a 'ring fence' (*Love's Coming of Age*,

106–8). Like Hardy's visitants, Scudder is a disturber who injects life into the decaying confines of the Durhams' Wiltshire estate. He is 'an importation — part of the larger life that had come into Penge' (*M*, 162), and his emanation is purely Carpenterian. Maurice, awaking from a trans-sexual reverie, leaps to a window of Penge House with a cry of 'Come!', and the gamekeeper climbs into his bedroom. In a lyric entitled 'I hear thy call' Carpenter had demanded:

Take me, great Life — O take me, long-delaying,
Unloose these chains, unbind these clogs and fetters;
I hear thy call — so strange — Mysterious Being,
I hear thy call — I come.

The consummation of the affair in *Maurice* echoes another Carpenter lyric, 'Summer Heat', in which the lovers 'lie naked on the warm ground, and the ferns arch over them,/Out in the woods, and the sweet scent of fir-needles/Blends with the fragrant nearness of their bodies' (*Towards Democracy*, 376, 284). Despite his trade connexions Alec is identified with the free life of nature. His role as keeper enables the novel to project him as an avatar of Whitmanesque open-air existence — a man who, ignorant of the precepts of *Towards Democracy*, thereby embodies them. His relationship with Maurice emancipates Alec from bourgeois pretensions (he grumbles ambiguously that the woods 'contain no "openings" '), and prepares for his final manifestation as 'untamed son of the woods' (*M*, 192). Alec's bodily beauty and naturalness is Carpenterian: it is with the 'appearance of the perfected human form that the work of creation . . . completes itself' (*Civilisation*, 183–4). The young keeper illustrates Carpenter's third stage of evolution when 'primitive healthy folk' attain 'the sublime Consciousness of simple Being' (*The Art of Creation*, 234). In his unconscious zest Alec resembles other Forster characters such as Gino, young George Emerson, Stephen Wonham, each of whom has to bear the weight of Forster's clandestine longing for a return to nature associated with a frank sexuality. Carpenter extolled the benefits of sex 'in the open air, in touch with the great and abounding life of Nature', and contrasted it with life in 'closed and stuffy rooms, the symbols of mental darkness and morbidity' (*The Drama of Love and Death*, 51). Forster's novel is an attempt to articulate this creed in dramatic terms. Maurice emerges from the 'middle-middle classes', 'whose highest desire seemed shelter — continuous shelter — not a lair in the darkness to be reached against fear, but shelter everywhere and always.' Maurice repudiates such people since for them 'the existence of earth and sky is forgotten.' by seeking shelter 'from poverty and disease and violence and impoliteness' they also shut out joy (*M*, 190). In *Towards Democracy* Carpenter described how urban man:

In houses hiding, in huge gas-lighted offices and dens,
     in ponderous churches,
Beset with darkness, cowers;
And like some hunted criminal torments his brain
For fresh means of escape, continually;
Builds thicker higher walls . . .
Twixt him and that he fears;   (*Towards Democracy*, 377)

Maurice, with Alec's help, breaks down the walls and his efforts are rewarded with an opened out happy ending. Characterisation of Alec also reflects Butlerian theory of instinct: 'It is only those who are ignorant and uncultivated who can know anything at all in a proper sense of the words. Cultivation will breed in any man a certainty of the uncertainty even of his most assured convictions' (*Life and Habit*, 28). The deep certitude and grasp of reality of the unlettered attracted Forster; their passionate directness and freedom from convention spoke to his inmost desires. Himself certain only of uncertainty, hemmed in by matriarchal inhibitions, Forster seized upon Butlerian instinct and Carpenterian pantheism in the creation of his archetypal gamekeeper. As Butler had observed, it is 'those who do not know that they know so much who have the firmest grip of their knowledge' — that is to say, young men 'who live much in the open air' (*ibid.*, 34–5).

In another area of the novel Forster mulls over Butler's argument and satirises the ideological claims of pseudo-science. Maurice's treatment by hypnosis appears to originate in Butler's description of attempts to eradicate instinct through hypnotism and in the more general current debate as to whether sexual abnormalities were suggested or innate. Butler refers the reader to W.B. Carpenter's treatise on the matter. Forster may have turned up the book in connexion with his own or Maurice's predicament. It would have appealed to him, for it is written in a cool sceptical tone and gives a fairly comprehensive account of practices current at the time. Dr Carpenter was specially interested in reflexes under hypnotism, finding in this area a complex yet mechanistic explanation which linked man with the animals. He underpinned his biology of mind with a belief in the correlation of mental and vital forces which he felt would provide the basis for empirical study of the nebulous area of experience where mental and organic factors appeared to relate: feeling, habitual acts, illness, trance and insanity. This was what he termed the 'debatable ground' between metaphysics and physiology. By admitting the will into the equation of mechanical nervous causation, Dr Carpenter believed he rebutted charges of materialism. Scientific laws were men's strategies for order, and in this episode Forster uncovers the deceit of positivism in annexing sexual 'irregularity' to mental illness or abnormality. The homosexual becomes a case-history of a certain type of sexual nature which is thus elevated, in nineteenth-century inquiry, to the class of a new species — what has been termed 'a natural order of disorder' being formulated. This science of aberrations reproduced the morality of its time in its prohibitions, and worked beneath the cloak of evolution in warning of the dangers to the survival of individuals and species if 'perversions' went unchecked or uninvestigated.

Lasker Jones suggests hypnosis to Maurice in order to divine 'how deeply the tendency is rooted' (*M*, 158), just as Dr Carpenter examined 'the subjection of the mind to a dominant idea' under hypnotism (*Mesmerism*, 4). Although Maurice is phlegmatic he breaks down under hypnosis and appears suggestible (*M*, 159), thus endorsing Dr Carpenter's comment that 'in individuals of that excitable nervous temperament which is known as "hysterical" . . . the *expectation* of a certain result is often sufficient to evoke it' (*Mesmerism*, 12). The 'hysterical coma' described by Carpenter is reproduced in Maurice's first interview with Lasker Jones, and Forster may have derived this material from Carpenter's study. Maurice goes into a trance, and Lasker Jones explains the technique to him: ' "Mr Hall! I shall try to send you into a trance, and if I succeed I shall make suggestions to you which will (we hope) remain, and become part of your normal state when you wake. You are not to resist me" ' (*M*, 158). The analysis follows Carpenter, who remarks that in this state some of the senses 'are not only awake, but preternaturally impressible; so that the course of the somnambulist's thought may be completely directed by suggestions of any kind that can be conveyed from without through the sense-channels which still remain open' (*Mesmerism*, 18). Under the pressures of his own isolation, Forster achieves masterly insight into the way science abets the hegemony of a dominant ideology. Thus he describes how Maurice longs for 'the trance, wherein his personality would melt and be subtly re-formed' (*M*, 183), but the longed-for metamorphosis does not occur — Maurice's is a false act of desperation sympathetically presented. Dr Carpenter largely demolished the claims of hypnotism as treatment for nervous disorders, and in the novel the hollowness of empiricism, seedily personified by Lasker Jones, and earlier by Ducie and Dr Barry, are exposed. The hypnotist ineptly embodies the tendency within the period to treat sexual 'abnormalities' through the highly ordered structures of the confessional; scientific discourse, utilising all the paraphernalia of interrogation, personal history, free association and hypnosis, reinstated the confessional as a crucial technique for eroding personal freedom through codification, classification and control of desire. In fleeing to the rendezvous with Alec at the boathouse Maurice turns his back on the value-system which seeks to undermine the very roots of his personality in the specious name of normality, and embraces freedom, instinct and nature. Within the autonomy of the novel Darwin is routed by Whitman.

The ending of *Maurice* must work on the level of myth. Forster is in a dilemma here: history pertains to society, and art can only function truly within that historical continuum. But in *Maurice* the Forsterian play of social irony is suspended so that historically and socially defined man may emerge into a new order founded on liberating instinct and drawing on the sensuous vitality of the working-class — a myth enabling Forster to picture the type of poetic renewal posited in Edward Carpenter's call for 'a return to the more primitive, indispensable, and universal part of oneself'. The myth is projection of the writer's inmost self, and commits him to somehow 'faking' a transcendence of the contradictions between social being and consciousness and ironing out the dialectic between the vaunted withdrawal from the social world and the inescapably socialised quality of individual life. The Edwardian homosexual was made acutely aware that civilisation was built on renunciation of instinctual gratification, and the false marriages in Forster bear witness to the pain of adjustment. More deeply, *Maurice* rehearses again Carpenter's sense of dialectic between sex and social institutions, his use of homosexual relations as an analogy of the new fellowship, and his efforts to relate consciousness and external social relations. Literature which authenticates the validity of private over social experience is not axiomatically escapist. In *Maurice* overtly, as in his other novels covertly, Forster made such an authentication. Placing members of two classes in a personal relation which defies the reality of the socio-economic disposition is a way of asserting that where those forces are modified the two classes provide a human complementarity which creates genuine freedom. The orientation of *Maurice* was necessarily uniquely private: its audience consisted of members of a closed circle. The public which plays its part in the definition of literature was here excluded, and Forster did not seek the moral consensus which had deformed the structure of his earlier novels. In this respect the code of the work lies closest to the penumbra of the author's unconscious. The novelist, aware that socialism might dismiss the subjective personal quest, insists upon the quest as his affirmation of being human. His sympathies lay with Carpenter's utopian impulse, but he acknowledged in 1931 that the labour movement had taken 'another course' and that Carpenter's vision was of 'the place that is still nowhere'. The search for that place began in the recognition of both writers that the industrial revolution and division of labour had estranged man from the natural world. The distinction between them lies in the fact that *Towards Democracy* speaks about an art calling for social action, whereas in *Maurice* the reintegration could only be achieved by abandoning the 'prose of social relationships' for a type of poetic renewal. Yet it is a renewal which bears witness to what Freud designated the 'hard, irreducible, stubborn core of biological urgency' which reserves the right 'to judge the culture and resist and revive it'. Perception of life is related to composition of aesthetic form in Forster's plea for novels which would end with an 'opening out'. Whilst the need for repression both aesthetic and sexual was a crucial factor in Forster's make-up, and in his artistic method of subtle indirection, the last third of *Maurice* constitutes an imaginative attack on that repression, and a delineation of the contingent social world reclaimed by the artist's imagination. Maurice's predicament is a crisis of both sex and class; in choosing a working-class lover for his hero Forster registered his sense of that crisis and his necessarily unpolitical solution in human relations. The effort here is to clarify the distinction between the personal and the class individual, whilst allowing these embodiments substance as visualised as being of a piece with sexual freedom, and in this respect *Maurice* constitutes a coherent pattern of problems and replies. Indeed the ghostly and indeterminate finale of the novel hints at new social tendencies making themselves visible through individual lives.

The middle-class, its class and sexual relations, and the evolutionary model which underpinned that set, all these factors are put to the test in *Maurice*. Forster achieves rhythm and concordance through the 'faking' he was to praise in *Aspects of the Novel*, inventing through the freedom conferred on Alec and Maurice that which satisfied his aesthetic and sexual desires in moving them from the known and determined towards the unknown and free. In its balance of opposites, and the guarded lyricism of its closing pages, *Maurice* bore witness to Forster's belief that 'novels can solace us.' But because the author does not wish to accept the mechanistic or ethical implications of evolutionary thought the solace takes the form of flight from society. The social fabric is antithetically conceived, finished product rather than organism in change and stress, and the protagonists are thus confronted by an inert mass of established conditions rather than the evolutionary framework within which Lawrence's characters define themselves. The forces of change, submerged under heavy-handed symbolism in *Howards End* and rendered inert in *Maurice*, were to be triumphantly faced in *A Passage to India*. Nonetheless there is achieved mastery in Forster's secret homosexual novel. As Carpenter told Forster in 1914, the book ends 'on a major chord', an ending which, 'tho' improbable, is not impossible & is the one bit of real romance — which those who understand will love.'

4   The Widening Circle

Lawrence's relationship with evolutionary doctrine has been examined elsewhere.[1] The novels do not reveal debts to such a body of theory, rather is evolutionary thought a means to an end, which is the novels themselves. Darwinism, that is to say, may be seen as a myth which helps to generate the Lawrencean novel. Huxley's argument that living things 'have no inertia and tend to no equilibrium' (*Man's Place*, 250), is translated, in Lawrence's theory of fiction, into a gradual breakdown of traditional character typology. Lawrence held that the writer's prerogative was to 'stand right in the flux', and by 1912 he was complaining of critics who 'want me to have form: that means they want me to have *their* pernicious ossiferous skin-and-grief form, and I won't' (*Letters B*, 492). The writer's mind pervades the fiction and renders all characterisation new and tentative; in this way Lawrence defamiliarises his subject matter and increases the intensity of readerly perception. The realist assumption that there is a common phenomenal world gives way, taking with it the 'old stable *ego* — of the character' (*Letters M*, 282; 1914). Like the fiddle-bow drawn across the sanded tray, characterisation in the novel would begin to take 'lines unknown' under the effects both of the dominant exploratory consciousness of the author and of the reader's active participation as interpreter. The fictional character, no longer a set of attributes fixed to a proper name, sheds the fossilised accretions of 'personality' and moves towards a recognisably Lawrencean selfhood. This is what happens to Aaron Sisson:

Now at last, after years of struggle, he seemed suddenly to have dropped his mask on the floor, and broken it. His authentic self-describing passport, his complete and satisfactory idea of himself suddenly became a rag of paper . . . he sat now maskless and invisible.

(*AR*, 198)

As Engels observed, the concept of the individual dissolved under the impact of science into 'something purely relative'. Interpretation of the new life-prompting leads the artist to discard form in favour of flux, as Paul Morel seeks to capture the 'shimmering protoplasm' in his painting, rejecting shape as a 'dead crust' (*SL*, 189). This piercing of the crust of reality into the central life-flow is most fully accomplished in the sexuality which links human and non-human worlds within universal process. By discarding the shell of life, Paul and Clara, for instance, come to know that 'they were only grains in the tremendous heave that lifted every grass-blade its little height, and every tree, and living thing' (*ibid.*, 430–1). The experiment of renewing the self is carried furthest in Birkin's reflections: 'How could he say "I" when he was something new and unknown, not himself at all? This I, this old formula of the age, was a dead letter' (*WL*, 417). Birkin here strives to articulate the novelist's perception that language abuses the differentness of things and people in their internal nature, his sense that novelistic 'personality' or 'character' is a rhetorical figure unfolded to disguise or subvert this differentiation. Identification of analogies between persons or things, their collective existence under a single mass or type, the insistence on sameness, all arise erroneously from resemblance. Naming means fixity and deadness wrought through the manipulative powers of language. Evolution of the self demands the disintegration of 'identity', a process which Gerald cannot accept in his will-driven move towards extinction in *Women in Love*.

In *The Rainbow* Lawrence applies this evolutionary principle equally to an entire society. Freud described the work of culture as the replacement of the id by the ego; in the drama of the replacement of early Brangwen instinct by Ursula's 'struggle for verbal consciousness', Lawrence shows man evolving, making himself through language. The entire tendency of *The Rainbow* is encapsulated in Engel's dictum: 'First came labour; after it, and then side by side with it, articulate speech.' The process of identity-formation unconsciously undertaken by the successive generations of Brangwens shows man creating new worlds and negating old ones; the continuous recreation of the self under new social conditions is precisely what the novel proposes for its subject. Wishing to account for the contemporary impasse through the experiences of Ursula, in the course of preparing 'The Sisters' Lawrence came to realise that in order to explain the human problem it was necessary to return to origins. The patterning of *The Rainbow*, tracing a movement from family to village to town to city, arose out of the novelist's social and writing experience: man, liberated from the determinism of nature, evolves into a victim/agent of the new determinism of culture. The uniquely human phenomenon of culture is successfully achieved only through curtailment of spontaneity; the petrification of reality discerned in the mining community at Wiggiston is one by-product of such willed repression. Spencer had insisted that 'like evolving aggregates in general, societies show *integration*.' In turning this positivist thesis on its head, Lawrence seems rather to reflect Tönnies's thesis of movement from community to society. The early Brangwens inhabit a folk society, in which the emphasis falls upon a non-literate, affective and homogeneous collectivity. The passionate struggle into conscious being which ensues through Tom and Lydia, Will and Anna, and finally Ursula, results in a type of urbanised consciousness, secular and individualistic. Ursula is torn between the communal world of her forebears and the modern socialised consciousness of Skrebensky or her Uncle Tom. As Tönnies observed, the state is opposed 'in veiled hatred and contempt' to remnants of folk-culture, and the typical character thrown up by modern conditions is 'hasty and changeable through restless striving'.

The theme of a literary work may be framed as a hypothesis: a certain set of events is seen as not only a particular group of happenings but also a manifestation of an underlying principle. In *The Rainbow* the underlying principle is evolution, wrought through enrichment of consciousness. Art, Max Nordau held, 'vouchsafes the most refined and highest knowledge', 'the knowledge of the future . . . the quick and vigorous organism pregnant with the future' (*Degeneration*, 334). In tracing the process of human and social evolution in three generations of Brangwens, Lawrence adheres to his early notion that 'there is a great purpose which keeps the menagerie moving onward to better places, while the animals snap and rattle by the way' (*Letters B*, 57; 1908). The culmination of *The Rainbow*, its raison d'être, was to thrust Ursula into 'the advance-post of our time to blaze a path into the future', as the publisher's blurb, probably attributable to Lawrence, first phrased it. The identity of character and author, which shifts between authorial omniscience, limited viewpoint and 'stream of half-consciousness', is fused in the latter stages of the novel into a unison of character and author — Lawrence had declared himself sometime earlier to be 'at the tip of the years' (*Letters B*, 124; 1909). Yet Ursula's intellectual freedom and independence, reached through the dark night of Brinsley Street school and her relationship with Winifred Inger, Skrebensky and Schofield, represent not simply individual achievement. Writing on 'Education of the People' in 1918, Lawrence asserted that 'the whole sum of the mental content of mankind is never, and can never be more than a mere tithe of all the vast surging primal consciousness, the affective consciousness of mankind' (*Phoenix*, 629). The wave-like patterning of *The Rainbow*, derived from Spencer's *First Principles*, enables the novelist to vary his time-span from generalised states lasting perhaps for months to the experience of a few moments. Thus Lawrence displaces the traditional sense of chronological time with a rhythmic process which affords him the subtlest sensitivity to periodicity in natural and human life. In the introduction to his history book, Lawrence describes how 'life makes its own great gestures, of which men are the substance', and how human history is to be conceived as surging motions in which 'men sweep away upon a tide' (*Movements*, xxviii). It is in such a 'welling-up of unknown powers' (*ibid.*, xxvii) that Tom Brangwen is first borne up, in courtship and marriage, and then obliterated by the black waters, made to give place to a new generation. The notion that 'Every man shall be himself, shall have every opportunity to come to his own intrinsic fullness of being' within these arcs of experience (*Phoenix*, 603) is implicit in every line of *The Rainbow*.

Lawrence's version of European history imaged mankind as 'a huge old tree: there are deep roots that go down to the earth's centre, and there is the massive stem of primitive culture, where all men are very much alike' (*Movements*, 307). In the opening of *The Rainbow*, with its primal seethe of life, this 'massive stem' is made manifest; and in the development of the story the growths from this stem are traced out in consonance with what Lawrence was to learn later of human evolution in Tyler's *Primitive Culture* (*Letters M*, 446, 463; 1916). Tylor, in his Darwinian study of anthropology, sees the primitive state as 'an early condition of mankind, out of which the higher culture has gradually developed or evolved' (*Primitive Culture*, I, 28), and he seeks to treat myth as 'an organic product of mankind at large, in which individual, national, and even racial distinctions stand subordinate to universal qualities of the human mind' (*ibid.*, I, 376). Evolution, however, had come to be interpreted as a theory of struggle. The conflict between the generations and the sexes in Lawrence is related to Tylor's application of Darwinism in which the 'theory of ceaseless conflict' becomes 'a key to the physical and moral nature and course of the universe' (*ibid.*, II, 330–1). Tylor places emphasis on language as both carrier and block to evolution, holding that ethnography 'reasonably accounts at once for the immense power and the manifest weakness of language as a means of expressing modern educated thought, by treating it as an original product of low culture, gradually adapted by ages of evolution and selection, to answer more or less sufficiently the requirements of modern civilisation' (*ibid.*, I, 217). Within the evolutionary context delineated by *The Rainbow*, language, by gradually substituting itself for the actuality of the physical world, is a force working towards both socialisation and individualisation: industrial man, with his secularised consciousness, lives primarily in and through language and apart from nature. In the Hardy study written concurrently with *The Rainbow*, Lawrence argued that life would tend to 'continually and progressively differentiate itself.' 'Life starts crude and unspecified, a great Mass', but 'proceeds to evolve out of that mass ever more distinct and definite particular forms' which work towards 'the production of the infinite number of perfect individuals' (*Hardy*, 43). That sense of progression owes its conception to Spencer's theory of the advance from homogeneity to heterogeneity as outlined in *First Principles*, an advance presupposed in the Spencerean definition of evolution as change from incoherence into coherence and in the Lawrencean dictum that the 'real opposite of love is individuality.' Social change, under this theory, is gradual and cumulative, determined from within and wrought through structural differentiation. The simple, unspecialised and informal personal and work relations of Marsh Farm give place, in the time-structure of the novel, to the complex, specialised and formal relations of the modern town. The origin of life, Lawrence holds, is 'uniform, a great, unmoved, utterly homogeneous infinity' which is later 'stirred and resolved' into individuation (*ibid.*, 44). Early generations of Brangwens exist in such primal homogeneity, but the women, wearying of the male 'blood-intimacy', start to face 'outwards to where men moved dominant and creative' — a dominance and creativity peculiarly marked out by the language skills possessed by the local vicar who speaks 'the other, magic language' mirroring and creating 'a quickness and a range of being that made Brangwen, in his large geniality, seem dull and local' (*TR*, 9). It is education, 'this higher form of being', which the woman wishes to give her children so that they should 'learn the entry into the finer, more vivid circle of life' (*ibid.*, 10). Education, language and class are inextricably linked: together they bequeath that mastery over nature which the Brangwen woman desires for her offspring. This is the germ of the evolutionary process which culminates in Ursula's vision of the rainbow. It has aptly been said that the end of history is inscribed in its very origins, and the final movement of the novel announces itself with the determination of Ursula to 'make something of herself' by emerging out of 'nothingness and the undifferentiated mass' (*ibid.*, 283). The subject of the novel is the struggle towards verbal consciousness, the cost of the emergence of Brangwen instinct into full mental comprehension. The 'passionate struggle into conscious being' begins in the unconsciousness of the natural round of agrarian life. In the successive generations from Tom and Lydia the active self-evolving soul achieves its own 'incarnation'. *The Rainbow* does not posit a simple process of emergence from darkness and chaos into the light of rational self-awareness. On the contrary, the more fully evolved the individual the more totally does the mind register what Lawrence calls 'primary consciousness' or unconscious forces. As he puts it in the Hardy study, the further man goes, 'the more extended his consciousness, the more he realises the things that are not himself' (*Hardy*, 44). Art, Lawrence held, should create symbols which are both 'pulsations of the blood' and 'pure percepts of the mind'. *The Rainbow* is, among other things, the aesthetic record of such a striving towards symbolism, in its examination of the way generative rules of order emerge out of formlessness into discrete existence. The final end of this generative act is the discrete, alienated existence thrown up by industrialisation.

The dominant evolutionary principle is signalled early on by Tom's encounter with the foreigner at Matlock, an incident which causes him to acknowledge 'a life so different from what he knew' (*TR*, 25), and which flowers into his pursuit of 'the stranger', Lydia. During courtship Tom 'submitted to that which was happening to him, letting go his will, suffering the loss of himself, dormant always on the brink of ecstasy, like a creature evolving to a new birth' (*ibid.*, 39). Under the stress of love he holds himself 'submissive to the greater ordering' (*ibid.*, 40), and this dazed submission marks his life with Lydia. Contact with his brother's cultured mistress, with her easy command of Browning and Spencer, causes a revulsion from life at the Marsh: 'He was a clod-hopper and a boor, dull, stuck in the mud. More than ever he wanted to clamber out, to this visionary polite world' (*ibid.*, 91). The act of rising through cultural acquisition is denied to him and he enters 'another circle of existence' through the sensual connexion with his wife (*ibid.*, 95). The farmhouse becomes full of 'deep, inarticulate interchange' and Tom does not 'want to have things dragged into consciousness' (*ibid.*, 105). When Will appears, Tom accepts he is to be a man 'put apart with those whose life has no more developments' (*ibid.*, 128). Yet he feels immature and unfinished to the end, seeing himself at the wedding as 'a little, upright figure on a plain circled round with the immense, roaring sky' (*ibid.*, 135). In Tom, as later in Will, Lawrence traces the shifting, tentative relationship between a nearly feudal communal order and more complex forms of social and intellectual organisation. Whilst his way of life coincides with the settlement-type of his inheritance, stress, conflict and self-contradiction are registered in his marital relations and finally dissolved in the flood-scene. The marriage relationship here results in a hard-won maturity which is also a circumscribing of potentialities. The evolutionary emphasis of necessity now falls forward onto the next generation, and the sense of struggle is underlined by the chapter-heading, 'Anna Victrix'. The movement of the second generation laps outwards in concentric circles from the honeymoon retreat, where Will and Anna find themselves 'at the heart of eternity, whilst time roared far off . . . towards the rim' (*ibid.*, 145). The rim is associated with the 'rind of the world: houses, factories, trams' (*ibid.*, 150), beneath which Ursula will finally discern a generative principle. Will is unable to connect 'outer' and 'inner' and takes refuge in religious mysticism with its enclosed and muffled passion. Anna's childbearing places her 'in the hands of such a masterly force of life' (*ibid.*, 192); Will, on the contrary, is baffled by the onward impulsion of evolution, and marvels to think of 'naked, lurking savages' developing the ability to create the 'massive, ugly superstructure of a world of man upon a world

of nature' (*ibid.*, 193). For Anna personally, further developments are irrelevant. She relinquishes the 'adventure to the
unknown' in favour of 'another soul' who should 'stand upon
her as upon the threshold' (*ibid.*, 196). Anna's annihilation of
Will's mysticism in the cathedral leaves him 'uncreated',
compelled to continue 'in the old form', whilst for the wife, 'if
her soul had found no utterance, her womb had' (*ibid.*, 206).
Will, focussing his life upon Ursula, is left uncomfortably
aware of 'buds which were not ripe in him': 'there was a
darkness in him which he *could* not unfold, which would never
unfold in him' (*ibid.*, 210).

Lawrence's project in placing the weight of the last half of
the novel on Ursula is to examine the process of extending the
'possible consciousness'. The genealogical format of *The
Rainbow* enabled him to analyse the way a dominating type of
consciousness is translated into authorial vision, and is
identifiable by the recurrence of patterns of relationship.
Structure of ideas determines the range of literary forms
available. Such a structure must of its nature be inherently
contradictory and tensile; this accounts for the disjunctions of
style and meaning frequently remarked upon in *The Rainbow*,
and notably for the paradoxical treatment of growth and
disintegration within each generation, a paradox finally
centring on the Ursula–Skrebensky relationship. In his
analysis of this passion, Lawrence wrestles with different
kinds of reductive disintegration but fails to make them
cohere: the corrosive activity of Ursula on the moonlit beach,
the materialist corruption of industrial Wiggiston, the potency
of Skrebensky with its range of 'African' suggestion, the sterile
modernity of Winifred Inger, and the powerful threat of the
horses. It has been justly said that fictional endings often fail
not only to resolve tensions generated within the novel but
often create new ones. The final scene of *The Rainbow*, which
relies on the rhetoric of evolution for its effect, is the botched
result of Lawrence's adherence to an ideology which distorts
the material presented earlier to the reader. In place of the
mysteriously autonomous universe of previous sections — the

cow-shed scene, the marriage speech, the honeymoon, Anna's naked dance, the potato-planting — Lawrence imposes a false consciousness upon his heroine in a desire to force meaning from the text. Comprehension of a whole way of life in its changing vitality gives place to a programmatic demand for a Lawrencean new life:

And the rainbow stood on the earth. She knew that the sordid people who crept hard-scaled and separate on the face of the world's corruption were living still, that the rainbow was arched in their blood and would quiver to life in their spirit, that they would cast off their horny covering of disintegration, that new, clean, naked bodies would issue to a new germination, to a new growth, rising to the light and the wind and the clean rain of heaven. She saw in the rainbow the earth's new architecutre, the old, brittle corruption of houses and factories swept away, the world built up in a living fabric of Truth, fitting to the over-arching heaven.

(*TR*, 495–6)

Where in earlier generations, and in the career of Ursula herself, Lawrence achieved intensity of realisation through confrontation of contending forces, the ending represents the upsurge of ideology at the expense of realisation. But what the rainbow scene implies is that society is not to be merely a system of self-preservation, or an industrial organisation underpinned by social Darwinism. The criteria of competition and survival, which have produced the terraces of squalid cottages, are transcended by the concept of a good life which the image of the rainbow labours to make manifest. Some words from Lucács's *Theory of the Novel* help to focus the problems faced at this juncture by Ursula and her creator:

The process which constitutes the inner form of the novel is the problematic individual's journey to himself; the road from gloomy captivity in reality which merely exists, which is heterogeneous and is meaningless for the individual — the road from this to clear self-knowledge. When this self-knowledge is attained, the ideal that has been discovered does, it is true, appear in the midst of life as the meaning of life; but the division between is and ought is not transcended, and cannot be transcended in the sphere in which this is enacted, namely in the life-sphere of the novel.

Despite the local failure here in the text the genealogical structure of *The Rainbow* permits Lawrence a dialectical analysis of personal and impersonal forces: the family group is at once the key biological and social institution and the battleground of the sexes and generations. What evolves is not only the social context — the move from agrarian to urban — but also the range of individual values, the extension of 'possible consciousness' implied by the fact of the novel for both characters and author. The clash in *The Rainbow* between nature and culture is radical and complex: culture, as Ursula apprehends it, is a crucial economic weapon for liberation. But its acquisition is also a form of bondage. The tension issues in the move of the Brangwens away from manual labouring life connected with the soil towards the kind of work typified by Ursula's school-teaching— a movement of broad typicality within the historical situation. Education both supplements and subverts nature. Ursula's relationship with education dramatises Lawrence's perception of how the institutional world thrown up by industrialisation comes to take on an objective reality external to humanity and coercive in its potential. Ursula, representative of a younger generation than Mr Harby, sees that the educational programme of Brinsley Street is, in all its machine-like inhumanity, humanly produced. The system of education is a social and cultural phenomenon, and the processes which created it will enable man to reject it by deviating from programmes set up by others. The deviation which Ursula attempts engenders conflict both with her class and the headmaster, and she saves herself only at the expense of submission to the system heartlessly manipulated by both master and pupil. With the earlier generations at Marsh Farm, family conflicts are held together within the structure of yeoman-farming: the Brangwens are workers but also owners and masters, and their freedom is dependent on the ground of seasonal labour. Property relations and blood relations cohere within an economic order felt initially as timeless An isolated world seeks what is not itself, hence Tom's quest for a foreign mate and the emergence of the Brangwen clan into the evolutionary spiral. The discovery, in Lydia, of passion and personal intensity to an extent subverts the values of the known agrarian order through its sense of aristocratic otherness, and although Tom dies within that order it is not so easy for subsequent generations. The romance of Will and Anna exists in a social vacuum divorced from social relations; Will's work means nothing to him and even his wood-carving is abandoned in the struggle for sexual mastery. The opposition is not a naive one between romance and society, and yet the couple are felt as limited and enclosed by comparison with the earlier generation. The social evolution which results in Will becoming a handicraft instructor and rising in the world is bought at the cost of natural vitality and openness to experience. It is the atmosphere of close breeding and defeat which Ursula kicks against, and the stages of her rebellion enact the discovery of a new style of being. Whilst the class-basis of her perceptions is vital to her role, ultimately Ursula is felt as becoming déclassé through self-awareness. The destructive intimacy with Winifred Inger and Skrebensky bypasses the social in order to reach towards the cosmic. The problem Lawrence faced was to realise this quest in socially comprehensible terms, to make the mysterious impersonal energies of destruction and recreation readable. In her love adventures Ursula is pushed to the periphery of society, and interprets Brinsley Street school as a prison and college as a sham. Yet what is premised by her love for Skrebensky is a transformation of real social relations, a thrusting outwards of the threshold of 'possible consciousness' towards which the vision of the rainbow makes a tentative gesture. Lawrence's failure here, the one-sided annihilation of Skrebensky's dark force, and the upholding of Ursula's destructive powers, arises from the limits of what he could historically say and feel. It is in this crucial sense that *Women in Love* arises out of the matter of *The Rainbow*. The forces harnessed in the Ursula–Skrebenky relationship may be fully realised in something more than the life of the indivdiual, and this feeling gives rise to the reflections about industrial and pastoral England when the lovers are on the top of the downs. *The Rainbow* juxtaposes social and industrial arrangements not only with personal relations but also with an alternative sense of meaning. But the threshold of consciousness compels Lawrence to present his idealism metaphorically in a way which does some violence to the weight of meaning and lived reality of the text, by assimilating the world of industry back into the world of nature in the closing image of germination.

As Ursula perceives at college, the offered culture is a mirror-image of the industrial base. That mirror-image dominates her crucial conversation with Dr Frankstone, who espouses a pure materialism. In this exchange Lawrence rehearses, with masterful economy of implication, the claims of positivism. Positivist science, in Dr Frankstone's exposition, postulates that there is nothing to be apprehended apart from the 'reality' which it alone can investigate. The trenchant materialism of the positive approach expounded here subtly extends itself throughout a society in which the major distinction becomes that between 'public' and 'private' experience, so that the individual is only able to define his sense of self in terms of the authority of a public sector — hence Skrebensky's deep-rooted patriotism which becomes as alien to Ursula as Dr Frankstone's ignorance of mystery in natural creation. The alternatives to this rationalism — Skrebensky's passional corruption, the dark weight of the horses — are not fully articulated. Indeed Skrebensky is a victim of bifocal vision, simultaneously an agent of sensual release and model conformist social integer. Like Hardy's later characters, Skrebensky is torn between sexual and mental, primitive and advanced consciousness. The two elements tear his personality apart, whereas Ursula attains a unity of vision through acceptance of the twin strands of her being — what may be termed the Brangwen and the Polish strains temporarily resolved by the rainbow. Nowhere does Lawrence face up fully to the indissoluble mix of creation and dissolution. The corruption of Ursula's Uncle Tom and its historical projection onto Wiggiston is meant to be counter-balanced by the vitality of Ursula, but the currents of evolution and dissolution predicated by Spencer run a subterranean course here to surface in full contradictory power in *Women in Love*. In a sense the nub of the interchange between Ursula and Skrebensky is one of class: the 'natural' aristocrat enslaves and destroys the aristocrat by birth. Like Tess, Ursula is an aristocrat 'developed through generations to the belief in her own self-establishment' (*Hardy*, 97). Lawrence's intuitive sympathy with his heroine cannot mask the Strindbergian capacity for destruction expressed in her 'harpy's kiss' (*TR*, 480). Years earlier Lawrence had remarked on how some men 'seem to be born and ruthlessly destroyed', and had found 'unity of design' for the race but not for the 'wretched individual' (*Letters B*, 41; 1907). Ursula pits herself against her experience: she successfully rejects her father's inadequacy, her mother's fetid breeding, Winifred's perverse sexual nature, and the male principle in Skrebensky and Schofield. Both heroine and exploiter, she ends the novel spiritually isolated, awaiting deliverance. The long evolutionary spiral which is Lawrence's concern issues in the metaphysics of the ending. The 'possible consciousness' extends itself in the phase of the composition of *Women in Love* under the exigencies of war; in that novel the impossibility of social integration is inexorably marked out, but the note of frenzied division of self from society towards the close of *The Rainbow*, of Ursula as one saved in a world of the damned, anticipates an unpleasant strain in Lawrence's later art. The effect towards the close of the novel is of social and spiritual dislocation, a disjunction whose roots lie in Lawrence's contradictory perception of the evolutionary process.

Lawrence had written that 'in every race, the growing tip is the living idea' (*Movements*, 309), and his artistic concern to delineate Ursula as the 'growing tip' of the Brangwens was firmly grounded in evolutionary educational principles with which he had long been familiar. In his 1908 lecture, 'Art and the Individual', Lawrence cited the German theorist J.F. Herbart, referring to the thesis that 'the immediate goal of education is to gain a wide sympathy, in other words a *many-sided interest*' (*Phoenix II*, 221). Jessie Chambers recalled that she studied Adams's *Herbartian Psychology* at college, that Lawrence was interested, and that they read the book together (*Delavenay*, 690). Some of the evolutionary concepts adverted to in the 1908 talk, deriving from Herbart, may have fermented in Lawrence's imagination and surfaced when he conceived the generational story of the Brangwens. This would be borne out in the talk by his sense of a 'consistent purpose working through the whole natural world and human consciousness' and of men as 'unconscious agents in a great inscrutable purpose' which he designated 'evolution' (*Phoenix II*, 222, 223, 226). Spencer, also cited in the talk, had written that education 'should be a repetition of civilisation in little', and Ursula's career recapitulates, in its emergence from primary into advanced consciousness, both the racial type of Brangwen aspiration and the concomitant stresses and dislocations. Herbart held that life was an educational process which remained forever incomplete, and that the individual repeats in his personal history the development of the race. The mind, he argues, is the sum total of all ideas encountered, hence physical and social environment are crucial. The mind is a battleground of ideas which are grouped into 'apperception masses', and education is to be a 'gradual unfolding . . . from low to ever higher stages'. The young Ursula acknowledges herself to be 'a wavering, undefined sensibility only, without form or being' (*TR*, 335). As Herbart wrote, 'those who consider the human soul as a fixed and concrete object, will never understand the mutability of the human character.' In the sense that the three generations recapitulate racial history, *The Rainbow* may be termed Herbartian. The novel explores the effects upon the Brangwen consciousness of varying apperception masses; it is no coincidence that an earlier title, 'The Wedding Ring', was dismissed by Lawrence because of its associations with 'the closed circle'. Herbart defined his apperception masses as cliques of ideas found in the soul or 'dome' beneath which lies the 'limbo of unconsciousness'. In another metaphor, consciousness is seen as a wave; ideas on the crest of the wave are 'focal', and in the body of the wave 'marginal'. At a certain depth the wave is crossed transversely by a line termed the 'threshold of consciousness'. The creative possibilities of this image for Lawrence's explorations of consciousness need no stressing. The apperception masses present similar, disparate and contrary ideas in 'presentations' which 'work their way upwards against opposing presentations'. The formulation of ideology is therefore a matter of conflict between apperception masses in a Darwinian sense, so that 'obstacles to desires are an important element in the cultivation of the circle of thought' (*Science of Education*, 130). The concept of the 'circle of thought' is seminal to Herbart's thinking on education. Lawrence twice uses the phrase 'The Widening Circle' to head chapters delineating Ursula's developing experiences, and this Herbartian notion forms part of the structure of the novel. Ursula's 'developing rejection of the old forms' (*TR*, 355) re-enacts in each stage Herbart's thesis that the world is a 'rich open circle filled with manifold life' which the child 'will examine in all its parts' (*Science of Education*, 68). Indeed it is 'in the culture of the circle of thought [that] the main part of education lies' (*ibid.*, 214). Ursula's experiences from childhood upwards exemplify Herbart's belief that humanity 'educates itself continuously by the circle of thought which it begets' (*ibid.*, 93). By contrast with the 'educated, unsatisfied people' 'inwardly raging and mad' to whom Winifred introduces her (*TR*, 343), Ursula's life represents a self-creative expansion of the 'great brown circling halo' of her forebears (*TR*, 49). She is, in the words of the original blurb, 'the leading-shoot of the restless, fearless family, waiting at the advance-post of our time to blaze a path into the future'. Herbart had written that it is 'the horizon of the individual determined by his opportunities' which locates 'the starting-point of advancing culture' (*Science of Education*, 125). Part of this advancing culture, and one of the key apperception masses Ursula must encounter, is the legacy of industrialisation embodied in Wiggiston, and in the brittle corruption of her Uncle Tom, with his cynical devotion to 'serving the machine' (*TR*, 350). The weight of Ursula's (and Lawrence's) rejection here is consonant with Herbart's argument that 'when each individual cares only for *his* own business or avocation, and all besides is but means to this end, society is a machine, and each member of it keeps his life warm at a single spark, which may be extinguished, and then nothing remains but dismal coldness, satiety, and disgust' (*Science of Education*, 111). In Ursula's parallel rejection of the education system of a materialistic society, similarly, Herbartian theory provides an ironic counterpoint. When Ursula enters Brinsley Street school she thinks how she will be 'the gleaming sun of the school', under whose influence the children 'would blossom like little weeds' (*TR*, 367). Adams had stressed that the soul of the child 'is in the teacher's hands', inasmuch as 'the apperception masses can be made and modified by the teacher' (*Herbartian Psychology*, 73), and Herbart praised those 'who know how to cultivate in the youthful soul a large circle of thought' (*Science of Education*, 92). The Herbartian ideal of education of a 'many-sided interest' (*Herbartian Psychology*, 278) through the 'principle of interest' and inculcation of the 'act of attention' (*ibid*., 263, 256) is brutally parodied in Ursula's immolation in the 'prison' of the Ilkeston school, and in her grim realisation of her duty, 'the graceless task of compelling many children into one disciplined, mechanical set, reducing the whole set to an automatic state of obedience and attention, and then of commanding their acceptance of various pieces of knowledge' (*TR*, 382). Just so do the owners of the means of production, through agents like Mr Harby, subvert the very life-chances of the propertyless. The elementary school-teacher, Lawrence held, was 'caught between the upper and nether millstones of idealism and materialism, and every shred of natural pride is ground out of him' (*Phoenix*, 589–90). Adams commented that 'in the last resort all interest comes from within' (*Herbartian Psychology*, 273), and recommends a type of 'cosmic selfishness': 'Only in so far as a man makes the most of his nature does he fulfil his function in the organism of which he forms a part' (*ibid*., 278). In 'Art and the Individual' Lawrence referred to the increasing comprehension 'of the incorporation of the individual in the social body whose interests are large beyond his personal feelings'. Such an individual 'is a unit, working with others for a common welfare, like a cell in a complete body' (*Phoenix II*, 222). It is Ursula's task, in encountering successive apperception masses, to define her own nature and the grounds of her being in the conflict between rational social demands and 'another, stronger self that knew the darkness' (*TR*, 452). In this act of definition Lawrence goes beyond his earlier adherence to Herbartian theory of society as organism: Ursula recognises in a moment of heightened sensibility that the world of man is 'like a circle lighted by a lamp' outside which lies fear and darkness and wild beasts, and that recognition of such darkness would bring ostracism from her fellow-men (*TR*, 437–8). As Lawrence maintained in a revision to his 1908 paper, art leads man 'to the edge of the great darkness, where no word-lights twinkle'.

Herbart thought that 'each personality is and remains a chameleon, and as a consequence every character will often be found in a state of inward conflict' (*Science of Education*, 204). The adolescent personality is the 'liquid substance' out of which 'the character will hereafter crystallise' (*ibid.*, 215). The act of crystallisation makes up the drama of Ursula's career, and her final acceptance of the 'dark stream' within the public citizen (*TR*, 448) is embodied in the tense flanks of the horses. Her growing realisation of otherness, her reconciliation of 'outer' and 'inner' worlds adumbrated by the rainbow vision, is the measure of her freedom, a freedom which derived, as Herbart had argued, from a transcendence of the 'calculations of egoism' by the individual's sense of the 'aesthetic revelation of the world' (*Science of Education*, 69). The circle widens from the centre outwards to meet the world, as Ursula's liberation finds its objective correlative in the conjunction of industry and rainbow, the heroine both reflecting and rejecting the historically determined moment:

Man stands in the midst of nature; himself a part of her, her power streaming through his innermost self, he answering external force with *his* own according to *his* method, *his* nature, first thinking, then willing, then working. Through his will goes the chain of nature.

(*ibid.*, 75)

The Rainbow deals with human beings living in time, but

the temporal perspective is twofold, embracing historical change in the environment and evolutionary change in the species. In the final wave of evolution Ursula can discover no mode of relating to an outer world in which relationships are conducted institutionally. It is a world conceived in masculine terms: Lawrence identified the evolutionary writers of his youth with the male principle, and poetically described their conception of evolution as 'one spirit or principle starting at the far end of time, and lonelily traversing Time'. This is only one half of the truth for him; there are two principles, 'travelling always to meet, each step of each one lessening the distance between the two of them' (*Hardy*, 97). In making her the embodiment of the countervailing 'great living Principle', the realisation of Ursula draws heavily on Lawrence's conception of Tess, a figure who is 'always herself' but 'utterly out of her element and her times' as a result of her 'old descent' (*ibid.*, 97–8). As in Tess, the female principle in Ursula is 'indomitable, unchangeable', so that she remains 'utterly constant to herself', yet 'by long breeding, intact from mankind' (*ibid.*, 98), and specifically from Skrebensky, who carries within himself seeds from the Hardy essay, notably Lawrence's characterisation of the male principle as comprised 'of Abstraction, of Good, of Public Good, of the Community' (*ibid.*, 99). The system founded in industrialist capitalism blocks and threatens vitality at every point of growth and it is the evolutionary struggle into being which destroys Skrebensky, who can make no connexion between private and public man.

Ursula is in any case always seeking in her lunar encounters with the lover to venture beyond him into 'pure being'. As Frieda Lawrence observed, the feeling here is that a love affair must go beyond the couple towards a 'bigger, universal connexion' which sets itself 'against individualism'. The blood-intimacy of the early Brangwens, sought in vain with Skrebensky but fleetingly located in the bargee, is to be finally incorporated into Ursula's own vital being. The treatment in *The Rainbow* of 'woman becoming individual, self-responsible, taking her own initiative' (*Letters M*, 273; 1914) places the focus on the isolated individual. In his sister's copy of *The Rainbow* Lawrence amended the rainbow vision so as to make this emphasis: 'She knew that the fight was to the good. It was not to annihilation but at last to newness. She knew in the rainbow that the fight was to the good.' The newness is Ursula's reconciliation of outer and inner, her location within herself of the seeds of the objective world, what Lawrence would identify, in the *Fantasia*, as 'the strangeness and rainbow-change of ever-renewed creativeness'. The heroine, in the pattern of growth through repetition with variation leading to adaptation, represents a universal tendency of mankind, a tendency exemplified in the entire descent into history and acculturation of the Brangwens. The cathedral builders, Lawrence believed, did not say ' "out of my breast springs this cathedral" ' but rather, ' "in this vast whole I am a small part, I move and live and have my being" ' (*Letters M*, 302; 1914). The patterned backward and forward flow of the novel mirrors Lawrence's awareness that 'we derive from the unknown, and we result into the unknown. But for us the beginning is not the end, for us the two are not one' (*Phoenix*, 696). It is Ursula's fate, awaiting the new life with Birkin, when she will be 'unutterably distinguished and in unutterable conjunction', as Lawrence wrote in his poem 'Manifesto', to participate to the utmost in the evolution of self and society. If the final emphasis is on self, on the way the self controls its past and brings to light forces from the 'prehistory' of its own human community, *The Rainbow* has also solidly imagined the development of a whole phase of history through social evolution. The novel is a fine endorsement of Marx's belief that society in this phase is 'no solid crystal, but an organism capable of change'; an entity, that is to say, which with all its inherent contradictory forces, is felt to be 'constantly changing'.

1 See the author's *Lawrence and the Nature Tradition*, Harvester Press, 1980.

5   Gerald's Sense of an Ending

As an inspector of schools, Birkin's acquaintance with Herbartian theory may be taken as read. The Prologue to *Women in Love*, written in 1916, explains how Birkin had made 'a passionate study of education' only to come to the realisation that it was 'nothing but the process of building up, gradually, a complete unit of consciousness': cultivation, that is to say, of the circle of thought. Each unit of consciousness, Lawrence argues, 'is the living unit of the great social, religious, philosophic idea towards which mankind, like an organism seeking its final form, is laboriously growing.' That process of laborious growth is traced out in *The Rainbow*, where the unidimensional ordering of events has an air of necessity which comes to be replaced by the contingency which overwhelms *Women in Love*. In his Prologue Lawrence faces the possibility that mankind may now be going through 'a corresponding period of decay and decomposition', activities which must be allowed to 'take their own way'. It is this possibility, underlined by the fact of war, which animates *Women in Love* in its dualistic vision of decadence and renovation. The distinction between the two novels is acted out in their form: *Women in Love* deconstructs, in paradox and self-contradiction, the procedures 'of *The Rainbow*. In moving from one to the other Lawrence reinvents the novel: the gestation of the two books shows the writer not only extending his class-based view of change but also demonstrating mastery over his material at a moment of supreme social crisis. The deepening world-view is not imposed from without; it becomes the new structure through form. This project involves replacing diachronic by synchronic structure, the language of causality giving way to a mode which stresses parallelism. The analogies and successions of the earlier novel are abandoned in favour of a construction displaying depths and surfaces. Where *The Rainbow* had shown the individual and his society evolving through time, *Women in Love* would analyse a system possessed of stable and unstable elements functioning (or disfunctioning) at a critical moment. Stability and process both seek equilibrium. Lawrence here discards the traditional horizontal axis of realist fiction with its sense of before and after, its insistence on memory and imagination as shaping and unifying agencies, in favour of an axis of verticality. During the nineteenth century man and language came to be regarded as possessing a history which might be uncovered through the concept of evolution; yet pursuit of origins led only to recognition of change, of the primacy of form and relationship over substance. The form of *Women in Love*, with its rapid disjunctions between classes, locations and groups, and its kaleidoscopic handling of mood and tone, takes its shape from Lawrence's partial abandonment of the evolutionary consciousness for a fiction which deals with ends rather than becoming. The development of industrial society, etched in at the close of *The Rainbow*, now appears to curve away from a relatively straightforward class structure into a series of élites — aristocrats, intellectuals, captains of industry, artists and so on — not a monolithic establishment, but rather a ring of establishments tenuously yet definitely interconnected.

A society in dissolution is articulated through the new vertical structure in which characters strive to fulfil their 'highest' or 'lowest' potential in a landscape, physical and mental, which subtly deforms the Christian tripartite schema of hell, earth and heaven. *Women in Love* is not so much social panorama as surgical cross-section: the phenomena of culture anatomised display and make clear the deeper reality of a system of values which controls behaviour. Nor is the novel conceived as a quartet; rather does the book work through a system of complex multiple relationships, sets of interrelated characters being held in a dynamic of uneasy stability. It is a feature of a heterogeneous social structure that no relationship is discrete. Any individual will belong to a variety of groups and perform multiple roles within a wide circle of less intimate associates; the house-party or café society are symptomatic of the attenuation of the profound social links integrating man into the community in the opening pages of *The Rainbow*. Gerald Crich, for instance, functions clearly within this multiple framework. He is seen as son, brother, blood-brother, lover, employer, murderer and suicide. In each role he is unable radically to evolve, as the characters of *The Rainbow* have evolved, or even as Ursula and Birkin are confusedly felt to do here. Eternally fixed (and fixated) Gerald can only repeat the multiplicity of his roles in an agonised search for self, moving up and down the scale from Minette in the dissolute whirl of Bohemia, or the submarine depths of the lake or the mines, up to Hermione on the social and Gudrun on the Alpine heights. Essentially in *Women in Love* the sense of movement, process and individuation which informs *The Rainbow* ceases, and the later novel proceeds rather by articulation of relevant contexts suspended vertically. The sole exceptions to the fatal stasis are Ursula and Birkin: in characters such as Hermione, Sir Joshua or Halliday the ego is definable as reified proof of a succession of identifications, whilst Ursula and Birkin are presented, albeit in a muddled way, as existing within a sequence of tensions in a future-directed process. Lawrence has arrived at a form, a system of interrelationships, which mirrors or narrates Engels's explanation of how 'innumerable intersecting forces, an infinite series of parallelograms of forces' effect unconsciously the historical event arising out of conflict: the end-product, in this case the Great War, would be what no one has consciously willed. The distinction upon which the novel turns, dramatised in the ending, is that between Birkin, seeking through dissociation with contemporary society a way through to renewed being, and Gerald, powerful exponent of that society, one who represents 'the last stages of our social development, the human being become mechanical, absolved from all relation' (*Letters M*, 432; 1916). Gerald, portentously viewed by Birkin as 'an omen of the universal dissolution into whiteness and snow' (*WL*, 287), is imbued throughout with a 'strange sense of fatality', 'as if he were limited to one form of existence' (*ibid.*, 232). He is the man in whom power has subdued desire, the man thrown into existence by evolution compelled to fill his life with projects which leave him dissatisfied. The ego, Freud wrote, 'is like a man on horseback, who has to hold in check the superior strength of the horse.' The Arab mare held by Gerald's will at the railway crossing possesses multiple cultural significance, representing Gudrun's rebellious submission, the anarchic feeling of the miners reduced to instrumentality in service of the machine, and subjugation of feeling to will in the man himself. Gerald, one of Nietzsche's 'herd of blond beasts of prey, a race of conquerors and masters', embodies Lawrence's critique of a civilisation built out of repression and functioning through survival of the fittest.

In the transformation of Thomas Crich's face-to-face paternalism into impersonal bureaucracy, 'the subordination of every organic unit to the great mechanical purpose' (*WL*, 260), Lawrence masterfully individualises the size-effect in industrial organisation and suggests its deadly potential for producing the 'finest state of chaos' (*ibid.*, 260). 'The Industrial Magnate' displays utmost command in its depiction of industrial history, and may illuminatingly be read in conjunction with Weber's theory of social and economic organisation. The underlying drift of the chapter is in the direction posited by Weber's belief that, by the turn of the century, capitalism was so highly developed that it no longer required the foundation of ascetic Protestantism, but had attained a secular value-system of its own which he named 'economic rationality'. The distinction between Thomas Crich and his son bears this out: the father has 'been so constant to his lights, so constant to charity, and to his love for his neighbour', and is possessed of the belief that 'in Christ he was one with his workmen' who are 'unconsciously, his idol, his God made manifest' (*ibid.*, 241–2). Gerald's god, by contrast, is not altruism but mechanism: 'When the machine is the Godhead, and production or work is worship, then the most mechanical mind is purest and highest' (*ibid.*, 253–4). This is the fundamental source of opposition between father and son, a clash through which Lawrence actualises sociological theory. At the inception of industrial processes the prevailing ethos is one of dependence; the workers are regarded as children who, if they perform adequately, will be protected from vicissitudes. It is this patriarchy, so infuriating to his wife, which Crich practises in his patient attendance on beggars and pleaders, and his handouts of food to the needy. That such a fatherly posture is essentially self-serving is brutally revealed in the lock-out, when mine-workers are shot by the militia which simultaneously guards the Crich mansion. Paternal authority is replaced, in the dynamic of the chapter, by a social-Darwinian concept of struggle for existence which justifies, in Gerald's mind, his wielding absolute authority in the name of progress, efficiency and scientific management. The sentimental servant-master relationship which insidiously destroys human mutual recognition is forfeit to the new relationship based on honest and naked exploitation, the 'stream of miners flowing along', 'all moving subjugate to [Gerald's] will' (*ibid.*, 250). The old man has wanted mines which 'run on love', a concern in which he will be 'a father of loving kindness and sacrificial benevolence', yet he lives to hear colliers shouting at him about his 'thousands a year' (*ibid.*, 253, 255). The deception, and essentially self-deception, of his patriarchal vision of the mines as 'fields to produce bread and plenty' (*ibid.*, 252) stands painfully exposed before his death. Old Crich typifies Weberian 'patrimonial authority': his authority and economic rights are regarded as privately appropriated economic advantages; his desires and ambitions are 'expressions of purely personal whims', as Weber wrote; and highly trained technical staff are 'typically absent'. Weber demonstrated his expropriation of labour grew up in the modern economy. Characterised by progressive development of the market system, by the technical superiority and indispensability of a type of autocratic management oriented towards the market, such expropriation was reflected in the power rela-

tions of the entire society. The final stage of the long transition
to full-blown capitalism envisaged in Lawrence's chapter
takes the form, as Weber explained, of the mechanisation of
production forces whereby non-human means of production
become capital and workers become 'hands'. In laying hold of
the mines in his great vision, Gerald suddenly conceives 'the
pure instrumentality of mankind' (*ibid*., 250) and determines
to use this instrumentality to exploit the mineral deposits: 'for
this fight with matter, one must have perfect instruments in
perfect organisation, a mechanism so subtle and harmonious
in its workings that it represents the single mind of man' (*ibid*.,
256). The mind is Gerald's. As Weber wrote:

An inanimate machine is mind objectified. Only this provides it with the
power to force men into its service and to dominate their everyday working
life as completely as is actually the case in the factory. Objectified
intelligence is also that animate machine, the bureaucratic organisation.

The pretence of equality and democracy is discarded in the
joyful struggle with 'inert matter': 'What mattered was the
great social productive machine' (*WL*, 255). Whilst Gerald's
ruthless modernisation follows the course outlined in Weber's
analysis of the evolution from patrimonial to bureaucratic
authority, with its emphasis on 'the exercise of control on the
basis of knowledge', the demonic personality of the younger
Crich also possesses the stamp of Weber's third 'type', defined
as charismatic authority. The charismatic leader is set apart,
endowed with supernatural, superhuman, 'or at least specifically exceptional powers or qualities', and is felt to be
answering a 'call' or 'mission' just as Gerald answers the call to
impose his will on men and natural resources. The miners'
lives and conditions worsen under this regime: 'The joy went
out of their lives, the hope seemed to perish as they became
more and more mechanised' (*WL*, 259), yet they submit
almost ecstatically to his dominance. He is their 'high priest',
representing 'the religion they really felt': 'There was a new
world, a new order, strict, terrible, inhuman, but satisfying in
its very destructiveness' (*ibid*., 259–60). Acting 'almost like a

divinity', Gerald so perfects the system that he 'was hardly necessary any more' (*ibid.*, 261). The miners work under his substitutes, the 'set of really clever engineers' (*ibid.*, 260) with which he replaces his father's ageing appointees. Weber pointed out that bureaucratic authority was 'seldom without a head who had a personally charismatic status by heredity or office', and in Gerald's almost unconscious handing over of the reins of power Lawrence subtly represents both that routinisation of charismatic authority examined by the sociologist and the ultimate nullity of the exercise for Gerald himself. Modern capitalism, raising on high the values of efficiency and production, subverts some of the deepest values of western man, his sense of creativity and autonomy of action. Thus it is that towards the close of the chapter Gerald feels an existential terror, 'not knowing what he was', and seeking futile belief in books, work or women, all the while recognising 'that his mystic reason was breaking, giving way now, at this crisis' (*ibid.*, 261–2). The weight of meaning substantiated in 'The Industrial Magnate' allows the reader to recognise the source of crisis within the system as well as within the man. Lawrence's recognition of these facts allows him the fullest range here, in a chapter which powerfully records both the unity and the complexity of the historical process.

Gerald's will-driven dynamism is incapable of change or response to others, hence the failure of Birkin's proposal of blood-brotherhood. He flourishes at the cost of repression, and develops into one of those 'hysterical and neurasthenical' characters described by Nordau, a type who, by engendering degenerates, will 'end their race' (*Degeneration*, 541). Gerald's mother, herself a weird victim of modern consciousness, aptly warns her son, ' "You're hysterical, always were" ' (*WL*, 369), and this hysteria culminates in the murderous attack on Gudrun, an attack predicted by Birkin's diagnosis of an act mutually desired by murderer and murderee. The attempted strangulation identifies the lovers with those who, having fixed themselves 'in the old idea, will perish with the new life strangled unborn within them', as Lawrence explained in his 1919 Foreword. Gerald and Gudrun are thus differentiated from those who, like Birkin and Ursula, 'bring forth the new passion, the new idea' (*Phoenix II*, 276). In the final climb after his murder attempt Gerald feels exhausted: 'He wanted so to come to the end — he had had enough' (*WL*, 532). The death-scene dramatises Nordau's thesis that western civilisation suffered from fatigue which led to degeneration and hysteria, whilst the survival of Birkin and Ursula counterpoises against this Lawrence's personal instinct for survival. Degenerates, in Nordau's thesis, more closely resemble Loerke, being 'anti-social vermin' who would be killed off through 'the severity of the universal law of life' in the struggle with 'lusting beasts of prey', the 'men of will'. Such men, Nordau observed, give 'the impression of being hard and cold'. Lawrence's deeper evolutionary comprehension allows him boldly to rework this commonplace social-Darwinisn, to foresee the survival of the cunning, adaptive futurist at the expense of the repressed apostle of organised mechanism. The ironies run deep, for both men extol the machine, and both are inhabitants of a world of death. A complex of cultural and historical experience is imbedded in the bifurcated ending. In one sense Gerald's death is inevitable, and he accepts it with fearful pleasure, just as earlier Ursula has felt a gladness to think that 'whatever humanity did, it could not seze hold of the kingdom of death' (*WL*, 216). Gerald has failed to reconcile being for others and being in itself, and leads a tormented double life. His tragedy bears out the thesis that the novel is the supreme literary form of a world in which man never feels at home.

Yet death itself is only a stage, as Birkin believes, in a longer process. In the *Fantasia* Lawrence was to extol 'the human potentiality to evolve something magnificent out of a renewed chaos'. In similar vein Birkin preaches to Ursula about the 'many stages of pure degradation' through which mankind must go 'in progressive devolution' (*WL*, 229), and elsewhere expounds his notion of 'universal dissolution' which 'ends in universal nothing' (*ibid.*, 193). The river of dissolution flows through both advanced and primitive civilisations, and is imagined equally in Gerald's glacial death and the West African carvings which fascinate and repel the mine-owner. When Birkin tells Gudrun that the carving of the savage woman in labour achieves 'an awful pitch of culture' and represents 'ultimate *physical* consciousness' (*ibid.*, 87), he is expounding directly from the Tylorian anthropology which Lawrence had just been reading. Tylor imagines 'primitives' turning upon their invaders and charging them with 'having fallen from the high level of savage knowledge' (*Primitive Culture*, I, 141). Lawrence's dramatised presentment of the disintegration of a culture is informed by both the Tylorian theory of 'high' civilisation carrying 'traces of the rudeness of its origins in ancient barbaric life' (*ibid.*, 246), and the Freudian concept of a tension between two selves created through the projection by a civilised sensibility of an inverted self-image — hence the cringing embarrassment of Halliday's cult of nudity. The complexity of the carvings, their fusion of high art and 'mindless' sensuality, may in its contradictoriness of suggestion exemplify the parallel which Freud drew between the dreaming mind which knows of no contradictions and primitive languages in which he held that one word could carry two opposing meanings. Cults of primitivism may be symptoms of cultural crisis, part of a more widespread atavism which finally welled up in the Great War: to that extent, *Women in Love* may be read as a work which supremely expresses the 'unity and collective rigour' of group aspiration and fear. As Birkin sees it, the incompleteness of both African and Nordic culture lies in their one-sidedness, the exaltation of some faculties at the expense of others. Wholeness in duality, Birkin's prescription for integration, is in his reading of the matter unknown alike to African and Nordic culture. The white races, Birkin predicts, 'would fulfil a mystery of ice-destructive knowledge, snow-abstract annihilation', whilst the West Africans 'had been fulfilled in sun-destruction, the putrescent mystery of sun-rays' (*WL*, 286). One of

Loerke's fantasies of the future with which he and Gudrun entertain themselves is of how the 'world went cold, and snow fell everywhere, and only white creatures, Polar bears, white foxes, and men like awful white snow-birds, persisted in ice-cruelty' (*ibid.*, 510). Gerald is by class and temperament a predator and exploiter who thrives on competition and the survival of the fittest: it is no mere accident that he should have killed his brother in youth, just as he kills off the spirit of the miners. The death of Gerald's sister, the blow to the rabbit, the brutality towards the horse, the attempt on Gudrun and the suicide represent hysterical repetitions of the killing of the brother, in itself a kind of self-murder. They are acts through which a partially assimilated shock tries to gain the threshold of consciousness. Indeed Gerald's successive careers as soldier, explorer, mine-owner and lover appear as a series of 'limit situations' through which he tries to define himself. Ultimately Gerald's exploitation of others recoils upon him as his will to survive fails of its object. Ruskin spoke of the 'cessation of all will' in the presence of mountains, and Gerald's will, broken by Gudrun's rejection and her cultivation of the troglodytic Loerke with his art of the future, finally lapses in the Alpine 'cul-de-sac'. His life is at a dead end. As Darwin observed, 'Not until we reach the extreme confines of life, in the arctic regions . . . will competition cease' (*The Origin*, 128) — the competition upon which Gerald has thrived.

More is involved here than a straightforward treatment of the fate of Gerald and mechanised organisation. The snow-bound scenes of *Women in Love* grow out of Lawrence's involvement with evolution as expressed in Spencer's theory of devolution. According to Spencer devolution counter-balanced evolution, which culminated in a lapsing away of life from the universe. The final pages of *First Principles* adumbrate the closing scenes of the novel. Dissolution is 'apt to occur when social evolution has ended and decay has begun', and social evolution, like biological forms, is dependent on a supply of energy 'which is gradually coming to an end' (*First Principles*, 416). Spencer's question, 'are we not manifestly

progressing towards omnipresent death?' (*ibid*., 413) leads to
a rhetorical flourish which foreshadows the ice world of
Loerke, Gudrun and Gerald:

> Does Evolution as a whole, like Evolution in detail, advance towards
> complete quiescence? Is that motionless state called death, which ends
> Evolution in organic bodies, typical of the universal death in which
> Evolution at large must end? And have we to contemplate as the outcome of
> things, a boundless space holding here and there extinct suns, fated to
> remain for ever without further change?
>
> (*ibid*., 423–4)

The shadow of such extinction hangs over the snow scenes of
Women in Love, with their pervasive sense of equilibration
sinking to dissolution in a drama of energy caught up in
irreversible degradation. Read within this perspective, the
novel stands as Lawrence's most trenchant critique, not only
of industrial society, but also of the idea of progress which
underpins and validates that society. Karl Kraus, giving
Spencer's Victorian apocalypse a modernist turn, remarked
that 'the modern end of the world will come about when
machines become perfect and, at the same time, man's
inability to function reveals itself.' In 'Education of the People'
Lawrence echoed this perception when he wrote of how man,
in 'disintegrating periods' of history, became 'a unit of
automatised existence' symbolised by 'the great man who
represents the wage-reality' who is 'hailed as the supreme'
(*Phoenix*, 609–10). This is what has happened to Gerald, and
it is pertinently asked where his 'go' goes to, since the energy
which reorganised the mines finally dissipates itself, leaving
him in 'an agony of inertia, like a machine that is without
power'. The machine has run down: 'Now, gradually, everything seemed to be stopping in him' (*WL*, 300). Laws of
evolution suggest unbroken continuity, but laws of physics
may hint at stopping or entropy. Under the second law of
thermodynamics energy dissipates into heat so that the
temperature tends to become the same everywhere within the
system and mankind is faced with thermal death. The total
amount of energy remains constant but becomes increasingly

less usable. Within a closed system there will be increasing disorder of energy moving at random, just as the particles of modern English life move randomly through the novel towards annihilation. Whilst torpor is actually a spread of momentum, to the observer it is experienced as a running down; it is the agony of the running down of a system that Lawrence records in *Women in Love*, the Will-to-Motion registered in *The Rainbow* giving way to the inseparable Will-to-Inertia. Cunning disorder of scene and dialogue enacts a larger disorder, just as the end of Gerald figures the end of the historical period of buoyant industrial capitalism. *The Golden Bough*, which Lawrence read in 1915, envisaged 'the sun someday cooling and we all freezing', but Gerald is frozen from the beginning and Gudrun is unwilling to unfreeze him or to release herself into creative autonomy. Aided and abetted by Loerke, her mode of dissolution remains negative, and is equivocally differentiated from the dissolution commended by the 'saviour' Birkin.

Birkin's form of consciousness is constantly superimposed against the prevailing institutional forms, but we note that this is achieved by virtue of his private income. The fixity of the soul is reduced in the river of dissolution back down to a kind of primal seething. Gerald organises the mines efficiently but the whole system verges on collapse through over-articulation, just as Gudrun disintegrates the 'vital organic body of life'. Lawrence described *Women in Love* as 'so end-of-the-world' (*Letters M*, 482; 1916), and announced, 'We have chosen our extinction in death, rather than our Consummation' (*ibid.*, 519; 1917). From the primal homogeneity of the early Brangwens, mankind's yearning for development culminates, at one level of meaning, on the Alpine heights. The yearning for development has issued in the industrialised consciousness so hideous to Ursula in *The Rainbow*, a type of mentality which focusses itself in Gerald. As Marx commented, 'consciousness of the past weighs like a nightmare on the brain of the living.' The characterisation of Gerald represents the Lawrencean critique of Spencer's theory of the gradual disappearance of imperfection, and his positivist claim that 'the ultimate development of the ideal man is logically certain': scientific materialism dies with Gerald in the snow of the abstract will.

Yet extinction is not the final note of the novel, in either form or substance. It is the tragedy of Gerald and Gudrun to grasp, like the conventional novel reader, at 'white finality' (*WL*, 461), and the mark of deliverance in Ursula and Birkin that they identify with the 'new, deep life trust' (*ibid.*, 540): in a world of process and becoming Lawrence locates corruption and hysteria with the demand for endings in life or fiction, denying the human capacity to 'fix absolutely the definite line of a book' (*Phoenix*, 308). Birkin, who early on is already 'thinking about race or national death' (*WL*, 33), foresees the end of humanity with joy, wishing it 'swept away': ' "If only man was swept off the face of the earth, creation would go on so marvellously, with a new start, non-human. Man is one of the mistakes of creation" ' (*ibid.*, 141–2). After recovering Gerald's frozen carcase, Birkin consoles himself with his evolutionary doctrine: 'Whatever the mystery which has brought forth man and the universe, it is a non-human mystery, it has its own great ends, man is not the criterion. Best leave it all to the vast, creative, non-human mystery. Best strive with oneself only, not with the universe' (*ibid.*, 538). Ursula, who justly suspects Birkin in his Salvator Mundi vein, might endorse the last remark, and the novel closes with quiet indeterminacy rather than evolutionary apocalypse; once again in Lawrencean fiction the ending marks a new beginning. Possessing Ursula, Birkin still feels keenly the loss of Gerald, and the failure of his homosexual programme of 'eternal union with a man,' 'another kind of love', that replacement of dyadic by triadic relations derided rather shrilly by Ursula as a 'perversity' (*ibid.*, 541). The balanced disagreement leaves the debate open to reformulation of the two kinds of love desiderated by Birkin, the firm singleness and melting union through which his nature might fulfil its needs. No man may exist alone, and in the relationsip of Birkin and Gerald Lawrence articulates his dualistic belief in the unity of opposites; the presence within Birkin's consciousness of a model, a rival, an opposite and an erotic object. Ursula, here in the final scene as in her appeal to Loerke for art to relate to life, sounds a humane note of survival and sanity in a world otherwise marked for destruction: instead of the new society envisioned at the end of *The Rainbow, Women in Love* posits the need for a non-social existence to be attained through the unlearning of man's cultural past. This novel, the culminating expression of the writer's concern with an evolving humanity, most deeply endorses his dictum that 'art-speech is the only speech'; it is here that Lawrence resolves imaginately contradictions he could not overcome in real life. The heightened intelligibility of art here transcends the muddle and confusion of war, of Lawrence's relationships, and his reactions to that war.

Yet it is Gerald, with his absolute demands on life and his passion for meaning, and not Birkin who functions as tragic hero. Killed in his prime, Gerald takes on himself a sacrificial role: a man personifying a late stage of industrial power and organisation through the dominance of the will, he is isolated by this very condition of representativeness, and is felt both to destroy himself and to be destroyed by 'reality'. Like earlier tragic heroes Gerald's excesses lead inevitably towards self-sacrifice, and the overtones of a perverse crucifixion take their place in the total effect. In this sense the final scene between Ursula and Birkin works like the close of a Shakespearean tragedy, both mourning the past and looking to a reconstructed future. *Women in Love*, indeed, vindicates the view that tragedy is an art founded in social tension and change. Nietzsche, speaking of the tragic poet, shows how he goes 'beyond terror and pity, to realise in fact the eternal delight of becoming'. This is an emotion Gerald's frozen carcase will never know: the delight of becoming carries over into Ursula and Birkin alone. Gerald, who has attempted through the will so to universalise his ego as to enslave competing life-forms, takes on in death the sacrificial role of the tragic hero.

Although his case is differentiated from that of Borkman, the fate of Ibsen's hero holds a proleptic significance for Gerald: the son of a miner, Borkman's obsession is to lay hold of the power of nature — 'the enormous mineral deposits! The quarries! The trade links!' 'All this', he asserts, 'I would have created alone.' Foiled of his wish to 'command all the sources of power', and of his need for redemption, Borkman retreats to die on the mountain heights, extolling the factories which are 'the outworks around the kingdom', the 'cold dark kingdom' of wealth buried within the 'ranging, soaring, towering peaks', until he drops dead, seized by the 'icy hand of iron'. The private corruption represented by Borkman's embezzlement, his own variant type of capitalist exploitation, is worked into a more universal deathliness in Lawrence's hero, who is similarly a pillar of society eaten away at the core of his being. Both Borkman and Gerald figuratively enact Engels's concept that history takes the form of transformation of positive forces into their negation: indeed, the classic instance cited by Engels is of the creation of an exploited and degraded mining proletariat out of the wealth of coal deposits and scientific inventiveness. Man, seeming to gain control of the world of matter, actually falls deeper into its power. Lawrence's recent anthropological studies had shown him how the hero could be killed off in order to prevent social disintegration or to compensate for communal failings. In exercising the possibilities of power Gerald becomes aware of its limitations as a mode of being. He desires power and lives to excess to confirm his own view of his stature, and within his life lie the seeds of his personal calvary. In the novel the figure of Gerald concentrates the feelings of power assertion; the apparent supremacy of his class and social group in fact acts as a limit to future development, so that at the end his death satisfies the opposing movement of feeling towards a surrender of the ego. Assertion and self-submission, the stuff of a tragic action, mark the life and death of Gerald, and his exalted self-immolation signals the end of one type of human evolution in Lawrencean fiction. In the snow-scene Gerald discovers the artistic comfort of closure:

faced by an alien world devoid of significant form, in a mirror-image of the activity of his creator, he imposes form through an ending, in this case his own.

Through Gerald, Lawrence conducts an exploration of the social determinants of consciousness: because of his class-affiliations Gerald can never understand or transcend the structure of capital which supports him, or see the possibilities for radical transformation with which Birkin, and the novel, are struggling. Industrial capitalism in this context is experienced in full contradiction: the miners are conscious of themselves as objects, selling their life-force to Gerald and other owners in exchange for commodity-production; the middle class, on the other hand, whether in the conversational arabesques of Breadalby or the bitchy gossip of the Pompadour, makes no contact with a world of things which exists only for their use or contemplation. Their tragedy, and Gerald's, is that they conceive the miners as the objects, and never the subjects, of history. The indirect relation of money and property to the objects of production is purely the consequence of the direct relation of the miners to those objects. It is this inertia, this distancing of self from a reified world, that Birkin tries to circumvent by visualising the world in evolutionary terms, an activity of coming into, or lapsing away from, being. His dislike and rejection of the 'Jane Austen' chair is symptomatic. It is nature, rather than what man has made, that is incomprehensible, a source of mystery welcome alike to Birkin and his creator. Lawrence's use of adversity in taking the war as crucial to the breakdown of routinised existence enables him to frame the image of human freedom, an image ultimately drawn from himself rather than his hero. In recounting a story of failure he succeeds, and the artistic success is brought about by conceiving the figure who is to be typical but never stereotypical. Gerald, that is to say, stands for the moment of history rather than any fixed element in society. The typicality thus achieved may be seen as an analogy between the plot — Gerald's conflicts with his father, Minette, Halliday, Gudrun, Birkin and Loerke — and the moment of history caught in its evolutionary trajectory. Lawrence, by virtue of his upbringing, was able to discern within himself the causal forces of his society. Lawrence's biography is of relevance solely insofar as he lives through, in his writing life, social transformations which he dramatises as a network of individual stories — narrative expressing most precisely the forces of social change and process which the author had experienced in Eastwood and beyond. The form which that narrative takes, in *Women in Love*, relates precisely to the aesthetic propounded in the Hardy study: the novel, that is to say, 'is a revelation of the two principles of Love and the Law in a state of conflict and yet reconciled.' In its seminal treatment of evolution and dissolution *Women in Love* discovers its form, magnificently dramatising what Lawrence designated 'active force meeting and overcoming and yet not overcoming inertia' (*Hardy*, 89).

Key to Texts Cited

(Place of publication is London unless otherwise stated)

Chapters 1 and 2

Hardy

CP:	*The Complete Poems of Thomas Hardy*, ed. J. Gibson, New Wessex edn, Macmillan, 1976.
Letters:	*The Collected Letters of Thomas Hardy*, Vol II, ed. R.L. Purdy and M. Millgate, Oxford: The Clarendon Press, 1980.
Life:	F.E. Hardy, *The Life of Thomas Hardy*, Macmillan, 1973.
Literary Notes:	*The Literary Notes of Thomas Hardy*, Vol I, ed. L. Björk, Goteburg: Acta Universitatis Gothoburgensis, 1974.
Notebooks:	*The Personal Notebooks of Thomas Hardy*, ed. R. Taylor, Macmillan, 1978.
Prose:	*Thomas Hardy's Personal Writings*, ed. H. Orel, Macmillan, 1967.
Novels:	New Wessex paperback edn, Macmillan, 1974–5, as follows:
DR:	*Desperate Remedies*
UGT:	*Under the Greenwood Tree*
PBE:	*A Pair of Blue Eyes*
FMC:	*Far from the Madding Crowd*
HE:	*The Hand of Ethelberta*
RN:	*The Return of the Native*
TM:	*The Trumpet Major*
AL:	*A Laodicean*
TT:	*Two on a Tower*
MC:	*The Mayor of Casterbridge*

TW:	*The Woodlanders*
TD:	*Tess of the d'Urbervilles*
WB:	*The Well-Beloved*
JO:	*Jude the Obscure*

Others

First Principles: Herbert Spencer, *First Principles*, Williams and Norgate, 1910.

Principles of
Biology: Herbert Spencer, *Principles of Biology*, 2 vols, Williams and Norgate, 1865, 1867.

Man's Place: T.H. Huxley, *Man's Place in Nature and Other Essays*, Dent Everyman edn, n.d.

The Origin: Charles Darwin, *The Origin of Species*, ed. J.W. Burrow, Harmondsworth: Penguin Books, 1970.

Chapter 3

Forster

Arctic Summer: *Arctic Summer and Other Fiction*, ed. E. Heine and O. Stallybrass, Abinger edn, Vol 9, Arnold, 1980.

Life: P.N. Furbank, *E.M. Forster: A Life*, 2nd edn, Secker and Warburg, 1979.

M: *Maurice*, Harmondsworth: Penguin Books, 1975.

Two Cheers: *Two Cheers for Democracy*, ed. O. Stallybrass, Abinger edn, Vol 11, Arnold, 1972.

Others

Life and Habit: Samuel Butler, *Life and Habit*, ed. R.A. Streatfeild, Fifield, 1910.

Mesmerism: W.B. Carpenter, *Mesmerism, Spiritualism etc. Historically and Scientifically Considered*, Longmans, Green, 1877.

*The Art of
Creation*:   Edward Carpenter, *The Art of Creation*,
Allen, 1904.

Civilisation: Edward Carpenter, *Civilisation, Its Cause
and Cure*, New York: Scribners, 1906.

*The Drama of
Love and
Death*:   Edward Carpenter, *The Drama of Love and
Death*, Allen, 1912.

*The Intermediate
Sex*:   Edward Carpenter, *The Intermediate Sex*,
Allen and Unwin, 1952.

*Love's Coming
of Age*:   Edward Carpenter, *Love's Coming of Age*,
Allen and Unwin, 1948.

*Towards
Democracy*:   Edward Carpenter, *Towards Democracy*,
Allen and Unwin, 1926.

Chapters 4 and 5

*Lawrence
Delavenay*:   E. Delavenay, *D.H. Lawrence: L'Homme et
le Genèse de son Oeuvre, Documents*, Paris:
Librairie C. Klincksieck, 1969.

Hardy: *Study of Thomas Hardy and Introduction
to these Paintings*, ed. J.V. Davies,
Heinemann Educational, 1973.

Letters B: *The Letters of D.H. Lawrence*, Vol I, ed.
J.T. Boulton, Cambridge: Cambridge University Press, 1979.

Letters M: *The Collected Letters of D.H. Lawrence*,
ed. H.T. Moore, Heinemann, 1977.

Movements: *Movements in European History*, ed. J.T.
Boulton, Oxford University Press, 1971.

Phoenix: *Phoenix*, ed. E.D. McDonald, Heinemann,
1961.

Phoenix II:	*Phoenix II*, ed. W. Roberts and H.T. Moore, Heinemann, 1968.
AR:	*Aaron's Rod*, Harmondsworth: Penguin Books, 1968.
SL:	*Sons and Lovers*, Harmondsworth: Penguin Books, 1971.
TR:	*The Rainbow*, Harmondsworth: Penguin Books, 1969.
WL:	*Women in Love*, Harmondsworth: Penguin Books, 1961.

Others
Herbartian
Psychology: John Adams, *The Herbartian Psychology Applied to Education*, Heath, 1915.

Science of
Education: J.F. Herbart, *The Science of Education*, trans. H.M. and E. Felkin, Swan Sonnenschein, 1897.

Degeneration: Max Nordau, *Degeneration*, Heinemann, 1895.

Primitive
Culture: E.B. Tylor, *Primitive Culture*, Murray, 1871.

Index

Wallace, A.R., 26, 30
Weber, M., xii, 99, 100, 101, 102
Weismann, A., 25, 26
 Essays upon Heredity, 26
Whitman, W., 67, 73

Yeats, W.B., 4

Zola, E., xx